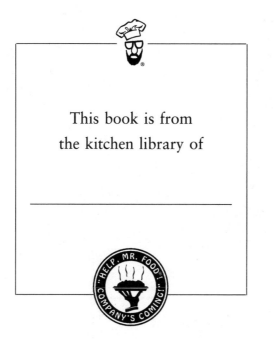

This book is from
the kitchen library of

_____

"HELP, Mr. Food®! COMPANY'S COMING!"

ALSO BY ART GINSBURG, MR. FOOD®

The Mr. Food® Cookbook, "OOH IT'S SO GOOD!!™" (1990)
Mr. Food® Cooks Like Mama (1992)
Mr. Food® Cooks Chicken (1993)
Mr. Food® Cooks Pasta (1993)
Mr. Food® Makes Dessert (1993)
Mr. Food® Cooks Real American (1994)
Mr. Food®'s Favorite Cookies (1994)
Mr. Food®'s Quick and Easy Side Dishes (1995)
Mr. Food® Grills It All in a Snap (1995)
Mr. Food®'s Fun Kitchen Tips and Shortcuts (and Recipes, Too!) (1995)
Mr. Food®'s Old World Cooking Made Easy (1995)

"HELP, Mr. Food®! COMPANY'S COMING!"

Art Ginsburg
Mr. Food®

WILLIAM MORROW AND COMPANY, INC.

New York

Library of Congress Cataloging-in-Publication Data

Ginsburg, Art.
"Help, Mr. Food®! company's coming!" / Art Ginsburg.
p. cm.
Includes index.
ISBN 0-688-14124-2
1. Entertaining. 2. Cookery. I. Title.
TX731.G52 1995
642'.4—dc20   95-32232
                                                                     CIP

Printed in the United States of America

2 3 4 5 6 7 8 9 10

BOOK DESIGN BY MICHAEL MENDELSOHN/DESIGN 2000

Dedicated to my wife, Ethel, and our family's firsts—
Steve, our firstborn,
Shayna, our first grandchild,
Jessie and Beth, our first (and only) twins,
Sam, our first (and only) grandson.

The children are *our* sources of entertainment—
and they give us the best reasons to celebrate!

Acknowledgments

Yippee! I finally did it! I wrote a book about my favorite pastime—entertaining! I'd always loved having company over so that I could surprise them with what I could whip up. So, when my wife, Ethel, and I became caterers, it felt totally natural. We had a successful catering business for over 18 years, and I've always brought a lot of what I learned and did during that time to my television show and cookbooks. But I'm thrilled that now I can really help you out by including topics—like easy party planning tips (page xvii)—that take a bit more time to explain but no more time to prepare.

Our children, Steve, Caryl, and Chuck, all worked with us in the catering business, and they help run our business today. I want to thank them for their commitment and their many contributions—past and present. My assistant, Howard Rosenthal, not only worked for us a bit during those years of catering, but founded and built his own successful catering business, which he recently sold in order to join the **Mr. Food®** team. I thank Howard for his dedication and for sharing his creativity with us now on a full-time basis.

Thanks, also, to all those who helped Ethel and me during those "building" years, and to those who support our current endeavors—from Flo, Carol, Roy, Tammy, and Patty to Tom, Joey, Laura, Alice, Monique, Marilyn, Beth, Fred, Stacey, and Laurie.

And we couldn't do all this without Bill Adler, Phyllis Heller, Michael Mendelsohn, and the team at William Morrow led by Al Marchioni. I appreciate you all!

I'm also grateful to all of my enthusiastic viewers and readers, and to the following companies and organizations who've provided helpful information and product suggestions:

Beatrice/Hunt-Wesson, Inc.

Dairy Management Inc.

Homemade Good News Magazine and Savannah Foods and Industries, Inc., makers of Dixie Crystals Sugar

Jana Brands, makers of frozen seafood products

Keebler®

M. E. Heuck Co., makers of Firm Grip™ kitchen tools

Modernage, Lauderhill, Florida

SACO Foods, Inc., makers of Real Semisweet Chocolate Chunks

Tryson House®, makers of flavor sprays

Villa Valenti Classic Sauce Company

Contents

Introduction

"Help, **Mr. Food**®! Company's coming! What should I do?!" Boy, do I hear this cry over and over as I travel around the country, and in tons of letters from my TV viewers. Well, your entertaining worries are over. Help is here!

I've got loads of ideas, recipes, and information inside to help you smoothly handle planned parties or spur-of-the-moment company. We all know it's no fun being stuck in the kitchen chopping, mixing, and preparing while everyone else is celebrating! So after you check out my entertaining helpers, you'll be ready for anything—and you'll be able to relax and enjoy your guests.

Oh, those Welcoming Appetizers! There are dips, spreads, and munchies from Home Run Dip (page 7) and Pizza Puffs (page 14) to Quick-as-a-Wink Shrimp (page 26) that can either be made in advance or be put together and on the table in no time. You might even want to serve a large selection of appetizers instead of a main course. That'll work great for a luncheon or other light occasion.

Then there's that marvelous meal—brunch. With easy make-ahead dishes like "Egg-cellent" Taco Brunch (page 55), Stuffed French Toast (page 44), and Breakfast Pizza (page 43), there are so many fun, yummy ways to satisfy in Brunch for a Bunch!

You know those times when you want to crowd around the kitchen table for dinner with your best friends? That's when Potluck Favorites are perfect. You can set everything on the table and let people serve themselves . . . and boy, will they love Finger Lickin'

Spareribs (page 86), Killer Kielbasa Chili (page 87), Chicken Rice Pie (page 67), and the rest!

We all have those times when special people come over and we want to serve something that'll really impress them. They'll go crazy over Apricot Mango Chicken (page 103), Stuffed Pork Chop "Roast" (page 124), Mustard-Glazed Tenderloin (page 121), or any of the Inviting Main Courses you make. And if you use some of my table-setting and easy garnish suggestions (page xxii), they'll be speechless!

Whether it's a casual meal or a meal to impress, you've got to have something to go with your main course. That's where my Entertaining Side Dishes come in. Parmesan Potato Sticks (page 143) go with almost everything, and so do Lovin' Onions (page 150). There are lots of other fun ways to dress up your special meals, too—like using fruit and unusual salads. You might want to make some Cheesy Hot Chicken Salad (page 176) or Shrimp Cocktail Salad (page 186), or even some Fruit Soup Plus (page 169) to make your meal memorable.

Okay, there are times when you don't need a full-blown meal. You know, like when the gang comes over to watch a football game. Whether your team wins or loses, you've got the tickets to making it a championship day with Jumbo Italian Meat Loaf Sandwich (page 191), Seafood Roll-ups (page 197), Baked Reuben (page 189), and more Crowd-Sized Sandwiches and Breads!

These days we're all busy, but we still want to spend quality time with our kids. Why not bring them into the kitchen and teach them while you cook? In Kid Stuff, I've got a selection of recipes that are fun to make and fun to eat (all except Play Clay, page 219—you can only *play* with that one!). There are Spaghetti Sundaes (page 206) and Waffle S'mores (page 213) and, if you're lucky, maybe they'll even share some of their Itsy Bitsy Pizza Bagels (page

210) with you! And when their friends come over, maybe you'll want to help them all make Mice Creams (page 214).

When you're having your own party, beverages are very important. No matter what the time of year or the occasion, most likely everyone will want something to drink during the event. That's why my Ice Breakers chapter is brimming with all types of tasty drinks, from Frozen Lemonade Cooler (page 232), Whiskey Sour Punch (page 227), and Nonalcoholic Frozen Piña Coladas (page 230) to Hot Mulled Fruit Cider (page 233) and even the frosty Brown Cow Milk Shake (page 235)! What toasting treats!

The most precious part of everyone getting together is that warm feeling of sharing. And you're going to be such a good host that nobody will ever want to say good-bye—at least not before having something sweet to top off the meal. So how 'bout sharing something really special for Sweet Good-byes like Triple Chocolate Cream Pie (page 271), All-in-One Carrot Cake (page 243) with Cream Cheese Frosting (page 244), or maybe a refreshing slice of Frozen ''Watermelon'' (page 272) or some Caramel Frozen Squares (page 245)? (I know—those will surely make leaving even tougher!)

Now I want you to make a promise—don't worry, it's an easy one. Promise you'll read my entertaining suggestions inside this book so that the next time you plan a party, get a call that the gang is on their way, or answer the door to find an unexpected mob of hungry friends, you'll relax and enjoy your company—'cause you'll know lots of ways to whip up plenty of **"OOH IT'S SO GOOD!!™"**

Party Planning Tips

So, you're having a party. Good for you! Let me help you by sharing some tips about what you should know (and you should keep these in mind whether you're planning months or hours in advance):

- **What's the occasion?**
  You'll be making your plans based on the reason for the celebration. Is it a birthday or anniversary party? A Super Bowl party? A shower, holiday get-together, New Year's Eve party, or maybe a Fourth of July picnic?

The answer will determine:

- **How many guests can you invite?**
  Whether it's going to be in your home or somewhere else, you need to be sure you've got enough room and enough seating for the number of people you plan to invite, depending upon how you plan to serve. (See the following information on buffet and sit-down meals.) If it's an outdoor party, you need an alternate plan for somewhere that'll comfortably fit all of your guests, as well as accommodate your kitchen needs, in case the weather doesn't cooperate.

- **What day, time, and season should you schedule it?**
  Remember, most parties last for 3 to 4 hours, so you probably won't want yours to start too late in the evening—unless it's New Year's Eve or some other time when you *want* to be up really late! A 75th birthday and a 50th anniversary party would

be the perfect occasions for a Sunday brunch because it's the best party time for people of all ages. You could serve a combination of the yummy make-ahead dishes from my Brunch for a Bunch chapter and add some bagels with specialty cream cheeses (pages 38 and 39). Or maybe you're planning an end-of-the-year holiday party. It's great to schedule it on Saturday evening so that families can join you and enjoy your twinkling holiday lights. If you've absolutely got to have an outdoor barbecue, obviously you should schedule it when the weather is most likely to be agreeable for outdoor events (but, as I said before, make sure you have a contingency plan).

- **Who will be attending and what should you serve?**
It's important to keep your guest list in mind when planning your location, time, and menu. Will you need a special menu—or maybe just a kid-pleasing main dish item like Farmers' Chicken Fingers (page 209) to make the younger ones happy? You'll probably want to serve something really hearty like an Explosive Deli Torpedo (page 194) for a Friday night poker game, and maybe more delicate Layered Sandwiches (page 195) for a ladies' luncheon. I've got a nonalcoholic Graduation Punch (page 228) that's perfect not only for graduation, but for a Sweet Sixteen party or any other time you need a festive drink. The type of food and how you plan to serve it will be determined by the answers to the above questions about the guest list, time of day, and location. Another factor is how much time you'll have to plan and prepare. If you use even a few of the tips and recipes here, you'll be done preparing before you know it—and your entertaining will be fun! Read on for my suggestions on how to become a party hero!

Planning a Perfect Buffet

The choice of whether or not to serve buffet style is up to you, but it's usually easier to serve a lot of people this way—even though it means presenting a larger variety of foods than you'd generally have for a sit-down meal. The better you know your guests and their food likes, the easier it'll be to know what to serve, but even if you don't know them too well, you can still offer enough choices to please everyone without it getting too complicated.

- Make certain that you have a good "traffic pattern." This will allow everyone to get through your buffet line as quickly and smoothly as possible. For example, don't put a buffet table in the corner of your kitchen. Try to keep it in the dining room or somewhere out of the main flow of party traffic. You'll need to get in and out of the kitchen often without having to maneuver around extra people!
- Place the plates at the beginning of the buffet table, where the guests will start serving themselves. Next should come a salad, followed by a main course, side dishes, bread, and, finally, dessert. If room doesn't allow for the dessert to be on the table along with the rest of the food, bring it out later during the party and serve it on a separate table or a countertop. Cold and hot beverages should be on a separate serving table or countertop, too, if possible. If not, have those at the end of the buffet table. And don't forget the silverware! I think the easiest way to put that out is to roll individual sets of utensils in napkins in advance and place them at the end of the buffet table so that people don't have to balance them all the way through the buffet line.
- Have a few cold foods and a few hot foods. That way there's a

variety for people to choose from—and having just a few dishes to warm helps when you have a limited amount of oven and stove-top space. Try not to put foods out too soon before serving time, and refill frequently.

- Serve foods that vary in flavor and texture. People like options. For example, offer two contrasting main dishes like Sunshine Chicken (page 106) and Mexican Fish Fillets (page 88) with Black Bean Salad (page 159) and Smashed Potatoes (page 139) on the side.
- Don't forget serving pieces! Every bowl or platter of food should have at least one serving piece—and be sure it's one that's appropriate, like a large spoon for meatballs, a slotted spoon for coleslaw, tongs for salad, a fork for cold cuts, etc.

Tips for Sit-Down Meals

Family-style or sit-down meals are still popular for smaller gatherings. Your sit-down meal can be casual or formal. You can dish out some of everything onto individual plates in the kitchen (the way

most restaurants serve). But my favorite way to serve is to set everything out in bowls or on platters for what's called family-style serving (that way everyone can take what and as much as he or she
wants). Here are some helpful tips:

- You should sit in the seat closest to the kitchen so that when
  you need to get up during the meal you won't disturb your
  guests.
- If you don't have enough room at just your kitchen or dining
  room table, it might be time to bring out your folding table. (We
  always called that extra table the "kids' table," and now I think
  it's flattering if I get to sit there!)
- Whether you use your everyday dishes, your fine china for a
  special occasion, or disposable paper- and plasticware for casual
  events, there should be a place setting for each guest. Be sure to
  have extras on hand, because you're bound to need something
  extra.
- You can choose not to cover your table (depending upon what
  your table is made of, of course), use a tablecloth, or use colorful
  place mats. (Don't forget to use table pads if you need them to
  protect your table from heat and moisture.) There are loads of
  different kinds, textures, and colors of paper and plastic plates,
  utensils, napkins, cups, tablecloths, and place mats available
  now. Some paper napkins even feel like linen. And if you want
  to use cloth napkins, they'll really make your guests feel special—
  and they're available in loads of colors and patterns now, too.
  It's easy to give your table a festive look!
- When setting your table, be sure to put out the right silverware
  for what you're serving—you know, a soup spoon if you're serving soup, a salad fork if you don't want your guests to use the
  same fork they'll use for dinner, etc. Here's my suggestion for a

proper place setting (if you're more comfortable doing it a different way, that's fine, too):

Dressing Our Food and Our Tables

There's an expression that says we "eat with our eyes." I happen to agree with that! No matter how good food tastes, it has to look good, too, or people won't want to eat it. Now, I'm not saying that we need to spend hours making fancy decorations or buy expensive table centerpieces. I just think we should go out of our way a bit to make our food and our tables look colorful when we're having company over. That might mean making a few simple garnishes or even just cutting your foods differently. Here are a few tips:

- Try accenting salads or other cold foods with thinly sliced cucumbers or lemons. And to make them look even fancier, before cutting, stripe the skin of washed cucumbers with a vegetable peeler or a fruit zester, or score the skin with a fork. Then slice away.

- Use cleaned parsley, scallions, or different types of lettuces or greens (the heartier types like endive, leaf lettuce, kale, romaine, and Salad Savoy are the best) for garnishing platters and individual plates. For example, it's easy to place a bit of green around a serving bowl and then place potato or macaroni salad in the bowl. Finish your garnishing by topping with a few cherry tomatoes, sliced hard-boiled eggs, or black or green olives. . . . Wow!

- Decorate with strawberries or radishes by cutting thin slices three quarters of the way through each and fanning them out. After cutting radishes this way, it's best to store them in icy cold water for about an hour so they really get a chance to "blossom."

- Great all-around toppers are fresh chopped parsley, scallion rings, and paprika. A sprinkle of any of them goes a long way.

- Fruit sure adds pizzazz! You can clean and cut almost any fruit into wedges or slices for adding quick color. Or get out your melon baller and garnish with melon balls. And you'll have a sure hit if you toss together 2 or 3 types of melon balls—maybe honeydew, cantaloupe, and watermelon—for serving in a watermelon basket. It's not hard to do, but if you'd rather keep it really simple, then maybe just cut a watermelon in half, scoop out and cut up the insides, then place the fruit back in the scooped-out watermelon "bowl" for serving.

- That same melon baller can be used for serving scoops of butter on top of pancakes, fish, or even for piling on a serving plate to go along with your favorite bread or rolls. Butter balls can be made in advance, laid out on a cookie sheet, covered with plastic wrap, and kept frozen until ready to use.

- Besides dressing up our food platters, we can fancy up our tables, too. You can buy an arrangement of flowers for a table center-piece, but a bunch of flowers loose in a vase are pretty, too (and usually less expensive). Fresh flowers are readily available these days—why, you can even pick some up while you're at the su-permarket. They sure add a fresh look and smell to a buffet or dinner table (but be sure they're not so tall that people can't see one another across a sit-down dinner table). You may want to make your own novelty decorations for placing around the house—and you can do this by using things that you've already got on hand. Drape a serape (a Mexican shawl) over a chair near your buffet table or put a piñata in the center of your Mexican buffet. Pumpkins, gourds, and baskets of apples sure say "Happy Harvest Time" on an autumn buffet. How 'bout putting party hats and streamers around the back edge of your New Year's or birthday buffet—or serve right from a wok on a Chinese buffet and add a few decorative Chinese fans around the back of the table. Just talking about this puts me in the partying mood!

- Don't forget the candles! They can create almost any mood—classy, romantic, or even festive. Just be sure to put something under them to catch drips, and place them safely out of the reach of little *and* big guests (and pets, too), and away from curtains, furniture, and other flammables.

Now go ahead and have fun making your party table special. I bet your guests will be surprised by what you can do—and so will you!

Notes from Mr. Food®

"Take-Alongs"

You'll notice that certain recipes throughout this book are marked with a 🧺. I call them my "take-alongs." They're foods that are just right for taking along to potluck dinners and for those times when you don't want to show up empty-handed at someone else's get-together. (Be sure to wrap them well and handle them safely during transportation.) For my list of "take-alongs" I've chosen a few dishes in each chapter that won't need any additional preparation when you get to where you're going. (Some simply need to be re-heated.) Watch how many smiles you'll help create!

Lighten Up . . . with Food Sprays

Throughout this book and in my other cookbooks, I frequently mention nonstick vegetable and baking sprays and recommend using them to coat cookware and bakeware before placing food in or on them. Here's why—these sprays are easy to use and, used as directed, they add no measurable amount of fat to our food, and now they're even available in nonaerosol *and* in flavored varieties! The flavored sprays are super ways to add a touch of taste, either before or after cooking foods, without adding lots of fat and calories.

Yields and Serving Sizes

Since this book is designed with company in mind, many of these recipes are geared for serving larger groups than my usual recipes do. But that doesn't mean that you can't use these for more intimate occasions, too. In fact, most of the recipes in this book can be easily adjusted to make larger or smaller quantities to fit your needs. Also, I like to serve generous portions myself, so I generally figure that way when I list the number of portions to expect from my recipes. Yes, appetites do vary and *you* know the special food loves of your eaters, so, as always, you be the judge of how much to make.

Packaged Foods

Packaged food sizes may vary by brand. Generally, the sizes indicated in these recipes are average sizes. If you can't find the exact package size listed in the ingredients, whatever package is closest in size will usually do the trick.

Welcoming Appetizers

I love to have company over to my house because when there's company, there's lots of special food! Sometimes we just feel like nibbling instead of having a whole meal. Maybe we want just a few hors d'oeuvres before dinner, or even as dinner by themselves. Why not? We all love munchies 'cause they're fun to eat and it gives us a chance to sample small portions of lots of different tastes.

This chapter is packed with all kinds of "starters" for lots of different occasions. It goes from Teriyaki Chicken Wings (page 23) and Creamy Crab Wontons (page 17), with an Asian flair, to a selection of my favorite dips. Those include a hot Bread Bowl Fondue (page 6), Back-Door Company Spread (page 8), and a quick throw-together called 1-2-3 Salsa Dip (page 9)—and they're perfect partners for a variety of chips, breads, and healthy fresh veggies!

Don't forget to put out my all-time favorite—a cheese board—with your appetizers. Buy special cheese or use whatever you've got on hand, from slices and chunks to spreadables. Mix different kinds, colors, shapes, and textures and serve them with a selection of crackers and some fresh fruit. . . . Wow!

For every occasion you can have a different appetizer selection—maybe "Off-the-Hook" Cocktail Spread (page 11) and Spinach Cheese Balls with Mustard Sauce (page 22) before a special dinner and Skewered Tortellini with Creamy Parmesan Dipping Sauce (page 24) and "TNT" Dip (page 4) before a barbecue on the back patio.

Spread 'em, dip 'em, serve 'em up hot or cold, but don't forget 'em! And the next time the doorbell rings, just relax and enjoy all the cheers of **"OOH IT'S SO GOOD!!™"**

WELCOMING APPETIZERS

 Mr. Food®'s "take-along" suggestion

Mr. Food®'s "take-along" suggestion

"TNT" Dip

8 cups

I got this recipe from a viewer in Texas who promised it'd be dynamite. Boy, was she right!

1½ pounds ground beef
1 can (10¾ ounces) cream of mushroom soup
¼ cup (½ stick) butter
2 pounds pasteurized processed cheese spread (like Velveeta®)
1 cup salsa
2 tablespoons chili powder

In a soup pot, cook the ground beef over medium heat for about 8 minutes, stirring frequently to completely brown the meat; drain the fat. Add the remaining ingredients and continue to cook over low heat until the cheese is melted, stirring occasionally.

NOTE: Serve with corn chips, tortilla chips, or party rye bread.

Hummus Pesto Dip

4 cups

There's a Middle Eastern dip called hummus that's becoming more and more popular in the United States today, and when it's combined with the garden-fresh taste of pesto, it's a combination that's sure to become your family's new favorite.

2 cans (15 to 19 ounces each) garbanzo beans (chick peas),
drained, and ¾ cup liquid reserved
4 cloves garlic
1 small sweet onion, cut into chunks
1 bunch parsley, cleaned, and stems removed
½ cup shelled walnuts
½ cup grated Parmesan cheese
¼ cup olive oil
1 tablespoon dried basil
1 teaspoon salt
¼ teaspoon pepper

Place the garbanzo beans and reserved liquid in a food processor and process until smooth. Add the remaining ingredients and process again until smooth and well mixed, scraping down the sides of the bowl as necessary.

NOTE: Serve cold or at room temperature with pita bread triangles or crackers.

Bread Bowl Fondue

5½ cups

Don't have a fondue pot? Don't worry! With this recipe you don't need a fondue pot for serving your cheesy concoction—only a hollowed-out rye bread. Yup, serve it right in the bread. (Now, doesn't that sound like the yummiest, easiest cleanup yet?!)

1 loaf (1 to 1½ pounds) plain rye bread, unsliced
2 cups (8 ounces) shredded Cheddar cheese
1 pint (16 ounces) sour cream
1 package (8 ounces) cream cheese
1 teaspoon Worcestershire sauce
1 cup diced scallions (7 to 8 scallions)
1 can (3 ounces) bacon bits
⅛ teaspoon cayenne pepper
¼ teaspoon caraway seed

Preheat the oven to 350°F. Using a serrated knife, cut the top off the bread loaf about one third of the way down; set top aside. Hollow out the inside, leaving about 1 inch of bread around the edges. Cut the bread that was removed from the inside into 1-inch cubes; spread out on a cookie sheet and set aside. In a large bowl, mix together the remaining ingredients until well blended. Put the mixture inside the hollowed-out loaf and replace the top. Double wrap in aluminum foil and bake for about 70 minutes. Toast the bread cubes in the oven during the last 15 minutes of baking, until crisp. Serve the baked loaf with the toasted bread cubes for dipping.

NOTE: Fresh cut veggies are super for dipping, too!

Home Run Dip

2¼ cups

Sometimes you want to make something for nibbling on when the gang is sitting around watching a ball game... Well, if you're looking for a home run, here it is!

3 cups (12 ounces) shredded Cheddar cheese
1 teaspoon dry mustard
⅔ cup beer
½ cup (1 stick) butter, slightly softened
1 teaspoon Worcestershire sauce
½ teaspoon hot pepper sauce
1 teaspoon onion powder
¼ teaspoon white pepper

Place the Cheddar cheese, dry mustard, beer, and butter in a food processor and process until creamy. Add the remaining ingredients and process until smooth and completely combined.

NOTE: Serve this at room temperature with crackers or cubes of Italian bread for dipping. It can be stored, covered, in the refrigerator for up to 2 weeks.

Back-Door Company Spread

4 cups

We all love having special company, but our regular drop-ins deserve something different once in a while, too—so try this one on your "back-door" gang!

2 packages (8 ounces each) cream cheese, softened
2 tablespoons milk
1 cup (½ pint) sour cream
2 tablespoons dried minced onion
1 jar (2¼ ounces) dried sliced beef, chopped (about ¾ cup)
½ cup chopped walnuts

Preheat the oven to 350°F. In a large bowl, blend the cream cheese and milk until creamy. Blend in the sour cream, then stir in the onion and dried beef. Spoon into a 1-quart casserole dish and sprinkle with the walnuts. Bake for 20 to 25 minutes or until heated through.

NOTE: Serve hot with unsalted crackers or party rye bread.

 Mr. Food®'s "take-along" suggestion

1-2-3 Salsa Dip

3 cups

1-2-3—yup, just three ingredients make this a great-tasting Tex-Mex dip ... in no time!

2 packages (8 ounces each) cream cheese
1 cup medium salsa
1 tablespoon dried parsley flakes

Preheat the oven to 350°F. In a medium-sized bowl, combine all of the ingredients and beat with an electric beater until smooth and well blended. Place in a 1-quart casserole or baking dish that has been coated with nonstick vegetable spray. Bake for 30 minutes or until lightly browned.

NOTE: Serve warm with tortilla chips or fresh cut veggies for dipping.

One-Dunk Spinach Curry Dip

2½ cups

I was at a party recently where I picked up a carrot stick and dipped into the dip. Nothing stayed on the carrot. I dunked again and still nothing came out! I knew I had to come up with a tasty sour cream dip that needs just one dunk.

1 package (10 ounces) frozen chopped spinach,
thawed and squeezed dry
1½ cups mayonnaise
⅔ cup sour cream
½ teaspoon curry powder
½ teaspoon onion powder
¼ teaspoon pepper

In a medium-sized bowl, combine all the ingredients; mix well. Serve immediately or cover and refrigerate until ready to use.

NOTE: Bring out all the fresh veggies—the carrots, cauliflower, celery, broccoli, bell peppers, mushrooms . . . yup, even the radishes and Brussels sprouts. Really—almost any fresh vegetable would love to be dipped in this winner!

"Off-the-Hook" Cocktail Spread

12 to 15 servings

Fishing through your recipes for a spread that will really hook your guests? Look no more, 'cause this is a winner in taste and presentation. If they fill up on this, you might even be off the hook for dinner!

2 pounds fresh or frozen whiting fillets, thawed and skinned
2 cups mayonnaise
½ teaspoon dried dill
½ teaspoon white pepper
⅛ teaspoon lemon juice
2 cups diced celery (4 stalks)
1 medium-sized red bell pepper, diced (about ⅔ cup)

continued

Snappy Cocktail Sauce
½ cup ketchup
2 tablespoons prepared horseradish, drained
¼ teaspoon dried dill
½ teaspoon lemon juice
½ teaspoon sugar
⅛ teaspoon salt

Preheat the oven to 400°F. Place the whiting on two 10" × 15" rimmed cookie sheets that have been coated with nonstick vegetable spray and bake for 15 to 18 minutes, until the fish flakes evenly with a fork; set aside to cool. Meanwhile, in a large bowl, combine the mayonnaise, ½ teaspoon dill, white pepper, and ⅛ teaspoon lemon juice; mix well. Flake the whiting into the mayonnaise mixture, picking out any bones. Add the celery and red pepper, mixing well. In a small bowl, combine all of the sauce ingredients and mix well.

NOTE: To serve, place the salad on a 10-inch serving plate and make an indentation in the center that's big enough to hold the cocktail sauce. Pour the sauce into the indentation. Cover and chill until ready to serve; serve with saltine crackers.

"Super" Bowl Dip

3½ cups

For years I've been sharing recipes that your gang eats up. With this one, I betcha they'll even eat the "bowl" it's served in!

1 pint (16 ounces) sour cream
1⅓ cups mayonnaise
2 tablespoons dried dill
2 tablespoons dried parsley flakes
2 tablespoons dried minced onion
1 jar (2.25 ounces) sliced dried beef, chopped (about ¾ cup)
2 round pumpernickel breads (1 pound each), unsliced

In a medium-sized bowl, mix all the ingredients together except the breads. Cover and refrigerate for at least 1 hour. Using a serrated knife, cut a hole in the top of one of the breads. Hollow out the bread, leaving 1 inch of bread around the sides, creating a bowl. Pour the dip mixture into the hollowed-out bread shell. Cut the second bread and the top and insides of the first one into 1-inch chunks and use for dipping.

NOTE: If you want to give your dippers a dark and light look, use 1 pumpernickel and 1 rye bread.

Pizza Puffs

10 puffs

Can you imagine the taste of pizza in a cocktail-sized puff? Here it is—and the taste is pizza parlor perfect!

1 package (10 ounces) refrigerated biscuits (10 biscuits)
¼ teaspoon dried oregano
¼ teaspoon garlic powder
Ten 1-inch cubes mozzarella cheese (5 ounces total)
1 to 2 tablespoons pizza or spaghetti sauce

Separate the dough into 10 biscuits. Make an indentation in the center of each piece with your thumb. Lightly sprinkle each indentation with oregano and garlic powder; top each with a cheese cube. Pull the dough over the cheese and firmly pinch the dough together so that the cheese is completely enclosed. (This is very important to prevent the cheese from oozing out during baking.) Place seam side down on a cookie sheet that has been coated with nonstick vegetable spray. Repeat with the remaining biscuits, seasonings, and cheese, placing the puffs on the sheet 2 inches apart. Lightly brush the tops with sauce. Preheat the oven to 375°F. Meanwhile, refrigerate the puffs for 15 minutes. Bake for 10 to 15 minutes, until golden.

NOTE: These are great make-ahead appetizers—just prepare them without baking and store in the refrigerator. Just before serving, bake as directed above.

Chinese Double Dippers

about 25 pieces

Be sure you serve these tidbits along with bowls of sweet-and-sour sauce and spicy mustard. (I think dunking them is the best part—and so will your company!)

1 pound boneless, skinless chicken breasts, cut into small chunks
1 can (8 ounces) bamboo shoots, drained and chopped
¼ cup all-purpose flour
3 tablespoons chopped scallion tops
2 tablespoons milk
4 teaspoons soy sauce
1 egg
¼ teaspoon ground ginger
½ teaspoon garlic powder
½ teaspoon pepper
½ teaspoon sesame oil
3 tablespoons vegetable oil, or more as needed

In a large bowl, combine all the ingredients except the vegetable oil. In a large skillet, heat the vegetable oil over medium-high heat. Fry heaping teaspoonfuls of the chicken mixture in the oil, about 10 at a time, for 3 to 5 minutes per side, until golden brown on all sides. Drain on paper towels and serve.

NOTE: If you want to fry these in advance, you can do that. Just cover and refrigerate them, then pop them in a warmed oven for a few minutes, and serve.

Garden Squares

32 squares

When you're in a hurry to make something garden fresh, these are perfect! Just mix 'em and bake 'em to feed to your hungry crowd!

1 cup biscuit baking mix
4 eggs
½ cup vegetable oil
½ cup chopped onion
½ cup grated Parmesan cheese
2 tablespoons chopped fresh parsley
½ teaspoon garlic powder
½ teaspoon dried oregano
½ teaspoon salt
¼ teaspoon pepper
3 cups sliced zucchini (2 to 3 small zucchini)

Preheat the oven to 350°F. Place the biscuit baking mix in a large bowl, then mix in the remaining ingredients except the zucchini. Fold in the zucchini, then distribute the mixture evenly in a 9" × 13" baking dish that has been coated with nonstick vegetable spray. Bake for 30 to 35 minutes or until golden. Allow to cool slightly, then cut into 32 squares and serve, or chill and rewarm just before serving.

NOTE: This is great as is, but why not try adding some dried basil, dill, or your favorite seasonings? And how 'bout serving these with spaghetti sauce or your own favorite dipping sauces?

Creamy Crab Wontons

30 wontons

When you get the word that the gang is stopping by and you want something to really impress them, just whip up a batch of these.

1 package (8 ounces) cream cheese, softened
¼ cup dry bread crumbs
½ teaspoon garlic powder
2 cups chopped imitation crabmeat (about ¾ pound)
30 refrigerated wonton wrappers (½ pound)

Preheat the oven to 350°F. In a medium-sized bowl, combine the cream cheese, bread crumbs, and garlic powder; mix well with an electric beater. Add the crabmeat, stirring until thoroughly mixed. Place 1 teaspoon of the crab mixture in the center of each wonton. Brush the edges lightly with water, then fold in half (one point to an opposite point, like a turnover) over the crab mixture, and press to seal. Place on a cookie sheet that has been coated with nonstick vegetable spray. Bake for 20 to 25 minutes, until crisp and golden brown, turning once halfway through the baking.

NOTE: Wonton skins can be found in your supermarket produce department and also in Asian food stores.

Wing Dingers

50 to 55 split wings

What do football season, after-school snacks, and birthday celebrations have in common? They're all perfect times for enjoying Wing Dingers!

5 pounds split chicken wings or drumettes, thawed if frozen
2 envelopes (from a 2-ounce box) onion soup mix
1 cup molasses
½ cup soy sauce
½ cup salsa
3 teaspoons hot pepper sauce
½ cup lemon juice
1 teaspoon garlic powder

Preheat the oven to 425°F. On two 10" × 15" rimmed cookie sheets that have been lined with aluminum foil, bake the wings for 30 minutes; drain any excess liquid. In a large bowl, combine the remaining ingredients, mixing well. Add the wings and toss until well coated. Replace the wings on the cookie sheets and bake for another 30 minutes, until the sauce begins to caramelize and the wings turn crispy.

NOTE: If you're a lover of really spicy wings, then another splash or two of hot pepper sauce will give these an extra zing. If you want to start with whole wings and split them yourself before cooking, split them at each joint and discard the tips. This makes them so much easier to eat.

Bacon and Cream Cheese Wedges

8 to 10 wedges

If you know a few days ahead of time that you'll be having company, these are your ticket to being ready when the doorbell rings!

¼ cup (1 ounce) bacon bits
1 unbaked 9-inch deep-dish pie shell
1 whole egg plus 3 egg yolks
1 package (8 ounces) cream cheese, softened
½ cup heavy cream
¼ teaspoon salt
¼ teaspoon white pepper
1 medium-sized tomato, cut into 14 thin wedges

Preheat the oven to 400°F. Spread the bacon bits evenly over the bottom of the pie shell. In a medium-sized bowl, beat the egg and egg yolks; add the cream cheese and continue beating until the mixture is smooth. Add the remaining ingredients, except the tomato wedges, and beat until well mixed. Pour the mixture over the bacon bits, then arrange the tomato wedges on top in a pinwheel pattern. Bake for 20 minutes, then reduce the heat to 350°F. and bake for 10 to 15 more minutes or until set. Allow to cool for 15 minutes before cutting into wedges.

NOTE: If you've got some leftover cooked bacon, this is a perfect way to use it up. Simply crumble it, and you're set!

Everybody's Favorite Meatballs

3 dozen cocktail-sized meatballs

I know that meatballs are a popular party hors d'oeuvre, and why not? They're easy to make and serve. But you know me—I like to make things my own way... so I came up with this new way to make cocktail meatballs with a punch!

1 can (2.8 ounces) French-fried onions
1½ pounds ground beef
1 package (0.87 ounces) brown gravy mix
2 eggs
1 bottle (8 ounces) ranch salad dressing

Preheat the oven to 350°F. Crush the French-fried onions in a food processor until they resemble bread crumbs. Place the crumbs in a large bowl and add the ground beef, gravy mix, and eggs; mix well. Form the mixture into 1-inch meatballs, about 1 tablespoon per meatball. Place on a baking sheet that has been coated with nonstick vegetable spray. Bake for 20 to 25 minutes or until the meatballs are cooked through. Serve with the ranch dressing as a dipping sauce.

NOTE: Serve these with toothpicks and watch them disappear!

Chicken and Broccoli Pizzas

two 11-inch pizzas

We sure have come a long way from the traditional sauce and cheese pizza... You may never go back after you taste this one!

3 tablespoons olive oil, divided
4 boneless, skinless chicken breast halves (1 to 1¼ pounds),
cut into 1-inch chunks
2 teaspoons garlic powder
2 teaspoons Italian seasoning, divided
Two 1-pound store-bought prepared pizza shells, thawed if frozen
1 package (10 ounces) frozen broccoli florets, thawed and drained
2 medium-sized tomatoes, chopped
2 cups (8 ounces) shredded mozzarella cheese
¼ cup grated Parmesan cheese

Preheat the oven to 400°F. In a medium-sized skillet, heat 1 tablespoon of the oil over medium-high heat and cook the chicken chunks for 6 to 8 minutes, until no pink remains. In a small bowl, combine the remaining oil, the garlic powder, and 1 teaspoon of the Italian seasoning. Brush each pizza shell with half of the oil and spice mixture. Spread half the broccoli, half the chicken chunks, half the tomatoes, half the mozzarella cheese, and half the Parmesan cheese over each pizza shell; sprinkle each shell with ½ teaspoon of the Italian seasoning. Bake for 15 minutes, until the cheese is melted and the crust is crisp and golden.

Spinach Cheese Balls

3 dozen

Our supermarket freezer cases are full of premade hors d'oeuvres and, sure, some are good, but why not make your own and really wow your guests? Just tell them you had a little help from **Mr. Food**®*!*

2 packages (10 ounces each) frozen spinach,
thawed and squeezed dry
2 cups herb stuffing mix, crushed
1 cup grated Parmesan cheese
⅛ teaspoon ground nutmeg
3 eggs
½ cup (1 stick) butter
½ cup finely chopped onion

Mustard Sauce
½ cup mayonnaise
¼ cup prepared yellow mustard
1 tablespoon honey

Preheat the oven to 350°F. In a large bowl, combine the spinach, crushed stuffing mix, Parmesan cheese, nutmeg, and eggs; set aside. In a medium-sized skillet, melt the butter over medium heat and sauté the onion until soft. Add the sautéed onion to the stuffing mixture and mix well. Shape the mixture into 1-inch balls and bake on an ungreased cookie sheet for 15 to 20 minutes, until golden and firm to the touch. In a small bowl, combine all of the sauce ingredients; mix well. Serve as a dipping sauce for the Spinach Cheese Balls.

Teriyaki Chicken Wings

50 to 55 split wings

Who says just because company comes over, you can't eat with your fingers? Not me! That's the best way to enjoy these wings!

¼ cup firmly packed brown sugar
1 tablespoon ground ginger
2 teaspoons garlic powder
½ cup dry white wine
1 bottle (10 ounces) soy sauce
5 pounds split chicken wings or drumettes, thawed if frozen

In a large bowl, combine all the ingredients except the chicken; mix well. Add the chicken wings and toss to coat. Cover and chill for 2 hours. Preheat the oven to 350°F. Drain the wings well and place on 2 large rimmed cookie sheets that have been coated with nonstick vegetable spray; discard the remaining marinade. Bake the wings for 30 minutes, then turn them over. Baste with the pan juices and bake for 30 more minutes, until the wings are cooked through and brown.

NOTE: These can marinate for up to 2 days in the fridge. That way when your guests arrive, you're ready for them. If you want to start with whole wings and split them yourself before cooking, split them at each joint and discard the tips. This makes them so much easier to eat.

Skewered Tortellini

40 to 45 skewers

There sure is something special about eating food served on a skewer. It's the same food, but it just seems to taste better . . . and your company will think you hired a fancy caterer!

40 to 45 six-inch wooden or metal skewers

1 bag (16 ounces) frozen cheese tortellini

Creamy Parmesan Dipping Sauce
½ cup mayonnaise
½ cup sour cream
½ cup grated Parmesan cheese
2 teaspoons pepper
2 tablespoons milk

Cook the tortellini according to the package directions; drain, rinse with cold water, and drain again. Place 3 tortellini on the end of each skewer. In a medium-sized bowl, combine all of the dip ingredients and mix well. Serve the cooled tortellini with the dip.

NOTE: To serve the tortellini warm, place the cooked tortellini on a rimmed cookie sheet with ½ cup water poured into the bottom, cover with aluminum foil, and heat for 15 minutes in a 350°F. oven. And to fancy these up a bit more, why not use tricolored tortellini? (You should be able to find them in your supermarket freezer case.)

Chili Dog Puffs

16 puffs

If you're expecting a crowd over to watch the game and want them to feel like they're right in the ballpark, here's how! I bet you'll almost hear the vendors shouting, "Chili dogs here! Get your chili dogs here!"

1 package (8 ounces) refrigerated crescent rolls (8 rolls)
½ cup (from a 15-ounce can) canned chili
2 hot dogs, each sliced into 8 equal pieces

Preheat the oven to 400°F. Separate the crescent rolls into 8 triangles. Cut each triangle in half crosswise, forming 16 triangles. Slightly stretch each triangle and place 1 teaspoon of the chili and 1 piece of hot dog in the middle of each. Bring all sides of the crescent rolls together and close completely. Place seam side down on an ungreased cookie sheet and bake for 10 to 12 minutes or until browned. Serve immediately.

NOTE: Serve these with spicy brown mustard.

Quick-as-a-Wink Shrimp

20 to 25 shrimp

Ding dong—the doorbell is ringing, and you need an appetizer in a flash! You can make this from start to finish in about 10 minutes. Is that quick enough?!

¼ cup (½ stick) butter
¼ teaspoon Italian seasoning
1 tablespoon light brown sugar
½ teaspoon garlic salt
¼ teaspoon cayenne pepper
1 pound large to jumbo raw shrimp, peeled, with tails left on,
and deveined (20 to 25 shrimp per pound)

In a large skillet, heat the butter over medium heat until melted. Add the Italian seasoning, brown sugar, garlic salt, and cayenne pepper. Stir in the shrimp and stir-fry for 4 to 5 minutes, until the shrimp turn pink. Do not overcook, or the shrimp will be tough. Place the shrimp on a serving dish and cover with the sauce from the skillet. Serve immediately.

NOTE: Shrimp are often sold according to the count per pound. I like to buy the ones that come 16 to 20 per pound or 20 to 25 per pound, but here's a great way to take advantage of whichever size is on sale.

Chicken Pockets

8 pockets

You know that surprised feeling of putting on a jacket and reaching into the pocket to find what you left in it the last time you wore it? You'll find a big treat when you check out these pockets!

1 teaspoon olive oil
2 boneless, skinless chicken breast halves (½ to ¾ pound), each cut lengthwise into 4 equal-sized strips
1 medium-sized red bell pepper, coarsely chopped (about 1 cup)
1 medium-sized onion, coarsely chopped (about 1 cup)
2 tablespoons dry taco seasoning mix
⅛ teaspoon black pepper
1 package (17.25 ounces) frozen puff pastry, thawed, each sheet cut into quarters

Preheat the oven to 400°F. In a medium-sized skillet, heat the oil over medium heat and sauté the chicken, red bell pepper, and onion for 8 to 10 minutes. Remove from the heat and add the taco seasoning mix and black pepper; stir and allow to cool slightly. Place 1 chicken strip in the center of each pastry sheet quarter. Divide the red peppers and onions evenly over the chicken strips. Fold each pastry piece in half and seal the edges with the tines of a fork. Place on a baking sheet that has been coated with nonstick vegetable spray, and bake for 20 to 25 minutes or until the pastry is browned and puffed.

NOTE: For a really special occasion, these make a great appetizer. Or cut each pocket into 4 pieces for a gangbuster hors d'oeuvre.

Sausage and Pepper Skewers

16 skewers

Sometimes we get so caught up in making fancy hors d'oeuvres that we forget what people like best. An all-time favorite is sausage and peppers, so why not serve them when company shows up?

16 six-inch wooden or metal skewers

1 red bell pepper, seeded and cut into eight 1-inch strips
1 green bell pepper, seeded and cut into eight 1-inch strips
1 pound Italian sausage, cut into sixteen 1-inch pieces
1 cup spaghetti sauce

If using wooden skewers, soak them in water for 15 to 20 minutes. Preheat the oven to 350°F. Thread each skewer through one end of a pepper strip. Thread a piece of sausage over each pepper, then curl the ends of the peppers over the sausage, pushing the skewers through the food to about ½ inch from each pointed end. Bake for 20 to 25 minutes or until the sausage is no longer pink. Just before serving, heat the spaghetti sauce in a small saucepan over medium heat for 6 to 8 minutes or until hot. Serve the sausage skewers on a platter with a bowl of warm sauce in the middle for dipping.

NOTE: Skewered hors d'oeuvres are really popular, and it's really easy to dip them into mustard or your favorite dipping sauces.

Cocktail Crab Cakes

28 to 30 cakes

You don't have to spend a whole lot of money on food when you want to invite friends over for a nibble. Here's an easy throw-together that makes them feel special ('cause they think you spent a fortune to make these).

2 tablespoons minced scallion tops
2 tablespoons mayonnaise
1 tablespoon Worcestershire sauce
½ teaspoon salt
¼ teaspoon cayenne pepper
3 eggs, lightly beaten
1⅛ cups dry bread crumbs
1 pound imitation crabmeat, flaked

Preheat the oven to 350°F. In a large bowl, combine the scallions, mayonnaise, Worcestershire sauce, salt, and cayenne pepper; mix well. Stir in the eggs and bread crumbs; add the crabmeat and mix well. Shape the mixture by tablespoonfuls into about 30 patties and place on a baking sheet that has been coated with nonstick vegetable spray. Bake for 12 to 15 minutes, until lightly browned.

NOTE: Of course you can make these ahead of time and warm them in a 300°F. oven for 10 minutes before serving.

 Mr. Food®'s "take-along" suggestion

Ham Croissant Melts

1 dozen small croissants

Remember the tuna melts and patty melts that most of us grew up on? Today we can make a quick snack that's a bit more special (and filling).

2 packages (6 ounces each) small frozen croissants (12 croissants), thawed
12 maraschino cherries
¼ cup prepared mustard
¾ pound thinly sliced ham
½ pound thinly sliced Swiss cheese, divided

Preheat the oven to 325°F. Slice the croissants in half lengthwise, separating the tops and bottoms; set aside. Process the cherries and mustard in a food processor or blender until the cherries are completely chopped and mixed with the mustard. Spread 1 side of each croissant with 1 teaspoon of the cherry-mustard mixture. Layer the ham and three quarters of the cheese evenly on the croissant bottoms. Cover with the croissant tops and top with the remaining cheese. Bake for 7 to 8 minutes or until the cheese is melted throughout. Serve immediately.

NOTE: Put these together ahead of time to the point of baking them. Then all you'll have to do is pop them in the oven just before you're ready to eat.

Sweet-and-Sour Meatballs

about 32 cocktail-sized meatballs

When I used to serve plain cocktail meatballs to the guys during football games, they'd eat 3 or 4 each, but now I make them sweet-and-sour style and each of them eats at least that many before kickoff!

2 pounds ground beef
1 egg
¼ cup dry bread crumbs
1 teaspoon salt
½ teaspoon onion powder
⅛ teaspoon pepper
1 jar (12 ounces) cocktail sauce
½ cup grape jelly
Juice of 1 lemon

In a large bowl, combine the ground beef, egg, bread crumbs, salt, onion powder, and pepper; mix well. Form into 1-inch meatballs and set aside. In a medium-sized saucepan, mix together the cocktail sauce, jelly, and lemon juice. Bring to a boil, then add the uncooked meatballs. Reduce the heat to low, cover, and simmer for 15 minutes, without stirring (so the meatballs can set). Stir gently, then simmer for 25 more minutes, stirring occasionally. Remove from the heat when the meatballs are cooked through.

NOTE: This recipe is best prepared the day before serving. Cover and refrigerate overnight; then skim the fat off the top and heat to serve.

Wrapped-up Kielbasa

30 pieces

In fancy restaurants they wrap tenderloin in bacon and call it filet mignon, and scallops in bacon to create a seafood brochette. Here I'm wrapping up kielbasa for an hors d'oeuvre I call yummy!

30 wooden toothpicks

1 pound kielbasa, cut into 30 ½-inch pieces
15 strips of bacon (about 1 pound), each strip
cut in half crosswise

Horseradish Mustard Sauce
½ cup prepared mustard
¼ cup prepared horseradish, drained
2 tablespoons mayonnaise

Preheat the oven to 375°F. Roll a piece of bacon around each piece of kielbasa and secure with a toothpick. Place on a rimmed cookie sheet and bake for 30 to 35 minutes or until the bacon is crisp. Drain the grease and discard. While the kielbasa pieces are baking, in a small bowl, combine the sauce ingredients and mix until creamy. Serve the sausage with the dipping sauce.

NOTE: These can be made a day or two before serving. Store, covered, in the refrigerator. Then all you have to do is uncover and warm them in a 250°F. oven for 15 to 20 minutes and serve!

Casino Clambake

8 to 10 servings

I used to visit friends who lived at the ocean, and they always made clams casino for me with fresh clams. They were delicious, but they sure seemed to take hours to make . . . and what a mess! I came up with a shortcut version that makes a super appetizer when company drops in.

3 cans (6½ ounces each) chopped clams, drained
2 cans (4 ounces each) mushroom stems and pieces, drained
1 medium-sized red bell pepper, chopped
1 medium-sized red onion, chopped
4 ounces bacon
¾ cup seasoned dry bread crumbs

Preheat the oven to 400°F. In a small bowl, combine the clams and mushrooms and pour evenly over the bottom of a 9-inch deep-dish pie plate. Process the pepper, onion, bacon, and bread crumbs in a food processor until smooth. Spread evenly over the clams and mushrooms. Bake for 20 to 25 minutes or until golden brown and hot throughout.

Brunch for a Bunch

For brunch at home the menu used to be your standard omelets and pancakes, which had you slaving over a hot stove at the last minute. Things sure are different today . . . and am I glad!

When you're planning on overnight company, or people are coming over for a Sunday morning get-together, here you go! I've got plenty of possibilities for you, including an awesome Egg and Cheese Biscuit Bake (page 40), a crowd-pleasing Breakfast Pizza (page 43), and surprising Stuffed French Toast (page 44). The best part about these recipes is that you can mix and match them. If you're expecting a small group, make just one or two. For a big crowd, make a bunch. That way everybody can choose their favorites, like Quiche Italiano (page 45), Hash for a Bash (page 46), Pancake Muffin Surprises (page 59), and more!

By preparing these brunch dishes ahead of time, you'll be able to enjoy your entertaining. Any way you look at it, brunch is coming back in a big way—and won't it be nice to be ready when company arrives at your door!

BRUNCH FOR A BUNCH

Mr. Food®'s "take-along" suggestion

Bagels and More

Wow! Bagels sure are more popular than ever—and I know why. Besides being so hearty, they're really versatile. I mean, they're great for snacks and sandwiches, and if you've got a basket of bagels and a few toppings, you're ready for a quick breakfast buffet with no cooking and no fussing—just lots of fun. And when you've got some flavored cream cheese to go with them, your breakfast, brunch, or meeting is bound to be a success. Check out the two on the following pages, but first be sure to read my bagel tips:

- **Be careful cutting bagels!** I suggest placing bagels on end on a cutting board and cutting carefully through them with a serrated knife. **Do not cut bagels while holding them in your hand! Do not put your finger in a bagel hole while cutting.**
- To warm bagels, place them on a cookie sheet and cover loosely with aluminum foil. Place in a 250°F. oven for 5 to 8 minutes or until warmed.

- Store cooled bagels in a resealable plastic storage bag on the kitchen counter or in the freezer until ready to use.
- Stale or dried bagels can be thinly cut and toasted on a cookie sheet in a 300°F. oven until dried and crispy. Serve the bagel chips in place of crackers with dips like 1-2-3 Salsa Dip (page 9) and Hummus Pesto Dip (page 5).

Raisin Walnut Cream Cheese

5 to 6 servings

1 package (8 ounces) cream cheese, softened
¼ cup raisins
¼ cup coarsely chopped walnuts

In a medium-sized bowl, beat the cream cheese with an electric beater until creamy. Add the raisins and walnuts and mix well. Serve immediately or cover and refrigerate until ready to use. Serve cold or at room temperature.

Vegetable Cream Cheese

5 to 6 servings

1 package (8 ounces) cream cheese, softened
1 tablespoon finely grated carrots
1 tablespoon finely chopped green bell pepper
1 tablespoon finely chopped onion

In a medium-sized bowl, beat the cream cheese with an electric beater until creamy. Stir in the remaining ingredients; mix well. Serve immediately or cover and refrigerate until ready to use. Serve cold or at room temperature.

Egg and Cheese Biscuit Bake

8 to 10 servings

You aren't gonna want to save this recipe for company—it's just so easy to mix it, bake it, and have a special breakfast on the table in no time. Why not try it this weekend? Treat your family like company!

1 large package (17.3 ounces) refrigerated buttermilk biscuits
(8 biscuits)
10 eggs
¼ cup milk
1 tablespoon dried chives
½ teaspoon salt
¼ teaspoon pepper
1¼ cups (5 ounces) shredded Cheddar cheese, divided

Preheat the oven to 375°F. Slice each biscuit into 6 pieces. In a large bowl, whisk together the eggs, milk, chives, salt, and pepper until well mixed. Stir ¾ cup of the cheese into the egg mixture. Add the biscuit pieces and toss to coat evenly. Pour the biscuit mixture into a 2½-quart casserole dish that has been coated with nonstick vegetable spray. Bake for 45 minutes or until the center is set. Sprinkle the remaining ½ cup of Cheddar cheese over the top and continue to bake just until the cheese is melted.

NOTE: This is best served right from the oven.

Baked Apple Pancake

9 to 12 servings

You ask the gang what they want for breakfast, and they say pancakes. They're not hard to make, but by the time you finish all the batches and you finally get to sit down, everybody else is practically done. No more! With this recipe you make one big pancake and cut it into pieces. It tastes the same, and now everybody gets to eat together. I think that's the best **"OOH IT'S SO GOOD!!™"**

2¼ cups prepared pancake and waffle mix
1½ cups milk
2 eggs
3 tablespoons sugar
1 tablespoon vegetable oil
1 teaspoon ground cinnamon
1½ cups cored, peeled, and chopped apples (about 2 small apples)

Preheat the oven to 425°F. In a large bowl, combine all the ingredients except the apples and beat well with a whisk. Stir the apples into the batter and pour into a 10" × 15" rimmed cookie sheet that has been coated with nonstick vegetable spray. Bake for 12 to 14 minutes or until the pancake is lightly browned on top. Cut into serving-sized pieces.

NOTE: Top these with butter and maple or pancake syrup. And if you want, go ahead and add fresh blueberries to the batter for even richer fruit flavor!

Sausage and Egg Muffins

12 servings

I love brunch, and I've got a new brunch favorite to share with you . . .

10 eggs
¼ teaspoon salt
⅛ teaspoon white pepper
¼ cup milk
6 frozen brown-and-serve sausages, thawed and cut in half
1 cup (4 ounces) shredded Cheddar cheese
½ teaspoon dried parsley flakes

Preheat the oven to 375°F. In a large bowl, beat the eggs, salt, pepper, and milk. Place each piece of sausage into its own cup of a muffin tin that has been coated with nonstick vegetable spray. Put 1 heaping tablespoon of cheese over each sausage piece, using all the cheese, then pour ¼ cup of the egg mixture into each muffin cup. Sprinkle some of the parsley over each muffin. Bake for 25 minutes or until a wooden toothpick inserted in the center comes out clean.

NOTE: For a really quick special breakfast, these delicious muffins can be made in advance. Just cover and refrigerate overnight for reheating the next morning!

Breakfast Pizza

6 to 8 servings

For years you've been telling the kids they can't have pizza for breakfast. We're allowed to change our minds, aren't we? I mean, can you imagine the looks on their faces when you tell them you made pizza for breakfast?!

6 eggs
¼ teaspoon salt
⅛ teaspoon pepper
3 tablespoons milk
1 tablespoon butter
One 1-pound store-bought prepared pizza shell, thawed if frozen
½ cup (1½ ounces) chopped pepperoni
½ cup (2 ounces) shredded Cheddar cheese

Preheat the oven to 450°F. In a large bowl, beat the eggs, salt, pepper, and milk. In a large skillet, melt the butter over medium-low heat. Add the egg mixture and scramble until firm, but not browned. Place the pizza shell on a pizza pan or large cookie sheet and spread the scrambled eggs over the shell; cover evenly with the pepperoni and cheese. Bake for 10 to 12 minutes, until the cheese is melted and the crust is crisp and golden.

NOTE: You can use bacon bits instead of pepperoni or mozzarella cheese instead of Cheddar—whatever you prefer.

Stuffed French Toast

8 servings

Looking for a fun addition to your breakfast repertoire? Not only will your French toast be stuffed . . . so will you!

16 slices white bread
4 ounces (½ of an 8-ounce package) cream cheese,
softened and divided
½ cup strawberry jelly, divided
5 eggs
3 tablespoons milk
2 tablespoons butter, divided

Spread 1 teaspoon of cream cheese onto each slice of bread, then spread 1 teaspoon of jelly over the cream cheese. Put the bread together, making 8 sandwiches. In a medium-sized bowl, combine the eggs and milk and beat with a fork. On a griddle or in a large skillet, heat one quarter of the butter over medium heat. Dip each sandwich into the egg mixture, coating both sides evenly. Place on the griddle and cook for 2 to 3 minutes per side, or until golden brown, adding more butter as necessary.

NOTE: Eat these just as they are or top them with maple or pancake syrup.

Quiche Italiano

6 to 8 servings

Quiche sure is a popular brunch selection, and when it's got a Mediterranean flair, it's a guaranteed winner.

One 9-inch frozen pie crust, thawed
1½ cups (6 ounces) shredded mozzarella cheese, divided
½ cup spaghetti sauce
⅓ cup (1 ounce) pepperoni slices
¼ cup chopped green bell pepper
¼ cup chopped onion
2 eggs
¾ cup heavy cream
¼ teaspoon each salt and black pepper

Preheat the oven to 350°F. Bake the pie crust for 6 to 8 minutes, until set; allow to cool. Layer the pie crust with ¾ cup of the cheese, then the spaghetti sauce, pepperoni, green pepper, onion, and remaining ¾ cup cheese. In a medium-sized bowl, combine the eggs, cream, salt, and pepper; mix thoroughly and pour over the filling. Place on a cookie sheet and bake for 45 to 50 minutes, or until the top is golden and a knife inserted in the center comes out clean. Cool for 15 minutes, then cut into wedges.

NOTE: Make a few at a time, wrap well, and freeze. Thaw overnight in the fridge and heat at 300°F. until hot in the center.

   Mr. Food®'s "take-along" suggestion

Hash for a Bash

6 to 8 servings

I remember a diner near the house where I grew up that used to serve the best hash and eggs. Mmm, mmm! Here's an easy way to bring back childhood memories . . . or make new ones!

½ cup (1 stick) butter
2 medium-sized onions, diced (about 2 cups)
1 pound frozen hash brown potato cubes, thawed
1 pound diced cooked corned beef (3 cups)
8 eggs

Preheat the oven to 350°F. In a large skillet, heat the butter over medium-high heat and sauté the onions for 3 to 4 minutes, until soft. Add the hash brown potatoes and cook for 10 to 12 minutes, stirring occasionally. Add the corned beef and cook for 5 to 6 minutes, until heated through. Place the mixture in a 9" × 13" baking dish that has been coated with nonstick vegetable spray and, with a serving-sized spoon, make 8 evenly spaced indentations about ½ inch deep in the mixture. Crack the eggs one at a time and place each egg in an indentation. Cover the dish with aluminum foil and bake for 20 to 25 minutes or until the eggs are cooked to your liking.

NOTE: I like to make the indentations in 2 rows with 4 indentations each. This way it's easy to scoop out in whole servings. You should be able to get a piece of whole corned beef from the supermarket deli department. And if you want to keep costs down, ask for the end pieces. They'll chop up just as well!

L.E.O. Omelet

8 to 10 servings

What does L.E.O. stand for? Anyone who's been to a New York–style deli for breakfast probably knows that it stands for lox, eggs, and onions—a real favorite. This version can be baked, so it's simple to serve and there's no last-minute messy cooking and cleanup.

18 eggs
½ cup milk
½ teaspoon salt
⅛ teaspoon white pepper
1 small onion, chopped (about ½ cup)
3 ounces smoked salmon, chopped or flaked (½ cup)
1 medium-sized green bell pepper, chopped

Preheat the oven to 350°F. In a large bowl, beat the eggs, milk, salt, and white pepper until well blended. Spread the onion, salmon, and green pepper evenly over the bottom of a 9" × 13" baking dish that has been coated with nonstick vegetable spray. Pour the egg mixture on top and bake for 30 to 35 minutes.

NOTE: This is another dish that can be made the night before your brunch and popped into the oven for reheating the next morning. (Just cover and refrigerate until ready to reheat.)

Cream Puff Shells

12 servings

Don't be fooled by the name—these shells aren't just for cream puffs. My favorite way to serve these is to fill them with a savory filling like shrimp or tuna salad (see the following page for a special tuna salad) for brunch. Of course, you can always fill 'em with ice cream for a fancy-looking dessert.

1 cup water
½ cup (1 stick) butter
¼ teaspoon salt
1 cup all-purpose flour
4 eggs, at room temperature

Preheat the oven to 400°F. In a medium-sized saucepan, bring the water, butter, and salt to a boil. Add the flour all at once and stir quickly with a wooden spoon until the mixture forms a ball. Remove from the heat. Add 1 egg to the mixture and beat hard with a wooden spoon to blend. Add the remaining eggs one at a time, beating well after each addition. Each egg must be completely blended in before the next egg is added. As you beat the mixture, it will change from an almost-curdled to a smooth appearance. When it is smooth, spoon out ¼ cup of dough for each pastry puff, spacing the puffs evenly on a large cookie sheet. Bake for 30 to 35 minutes, until golden and puffed. Cool on a wire rack.

NOTE: Cut each pastry puff in half crosswise and fill with scoops of your favorite fillings.

Dressed-up Tuna Salad

10 to 12 servings

Even the simplest foods can have a whole new taste with the addition of a few unique items...

3 cans (6.5 ounces each) tuna, well drained and flaked
¾ cup chopped celery (1 to 2 stalks)
½ cup mayonnaise
½ cup Italian dressing
2 tablespoons grated Parmesan cheese

In a large bowl, combine all the ingredients; mix well. Cover and chill until ready to use. Scoop into cream puff shells (page 48) and serve.

Tuna Salad

NOTE: Add some chopped red bell pepper or sliced black olives for extra festive color.

Canadian Breakfast Muffins

8 servings

No time to prepare for that last-minute drop-in company? In just 15 minutes you can be serving a breakfast treat that adults will love . . . and kids, too!

4 English muffins, split in half
2 medium-sized tomatoes, sliced
8 slices Canadian bacon (about 4 ounces total)
8 slices Muenster cheese (4 to 5 ounces total)

Preheat the broiler. Lay out the English muffins on a cookie sheet and toast them under the broiler for 3 to 5 minutes or until lightly browned. Layer each muffin half with a slice of tomato, Canadian bacon, then cheese. Turn off the broiler and turn on the oven to 350°F. Bake for 7 to 9 minutes, until the cheese is melted and the muffin is heated through.

NOTE: Canadian bacon can be found in the supermarket along with the regular bacon and pre-sliced meats.

Brunch Burritos

10 servings

When I first made these in our test kitchen, I couldn't believe the raves they got.... "Incredible!" and "awesome!" were just the beginning. How would you describe them?

10 eggs
½ cup milk
½ teaspoon salt
¼ teaspoon white pepper
2 tablespoons butter, divided
1 medium-sized onion, chopped (about 1 cup)
1 medium-sized green or red bell pepper, chopped (about 1 cup)
Ten 7-inch flour tortillas
2 cups medium salsa
1½ cups (6 ounces) shredded Colby-Jack cheese

Preheat the oven to 350°F. In a large bowl, beat the eggs, milk, salt, and white pepper until well mixed; set aside. In a large skillet, melt 1 tablespoon of the butter over medium heat. Add the onion and bell pepper and sauté for 6 to 8 minutes, until softened. Reduce the heat to medium-low; add the remaining tablespoon of butter and then the egg mixture. Cook the eggs until scrambled, but still moist. Spoon some of the egg mixture into the center of each tortilla and top each with a tablespoon of salsa. Roll up each tortilla and place in a 9" × 13" baking dish that has been coated with nonstick vegetable spray. Put 2 to 3 more tablespoons of salsa on top of each.

continued

Spread the cheese evenly over the tops of the burritos. Coat one side of a sheet of aluminum foil with nonstick vegetable spray and, with the coated side facing down, cover the tortillas. Bake for 25 minutes or until the cheese is melted and bubbly and the burritos are warmed through.

Overnight Success Soufflé

8 to 12 servings

Typically, when most people flip through a cookbook, they pass right by the soufflés because they think they're complicated and they will have to be so careful when making them. Not this one! You can make it up the night before your brunch, then bake it in the morning before your company arrives. They'll think you fussed all night!

16 slices (½-inch-thick) challah (egg bread) or white bread
3 cups (12 ounces) shredded Swiss cheese, divided
8 eggs
2½ cups milk
1 teaspoon dry mustard
2 teaspoons onion powder
½ teaspoon salt
½ teaspoon pepper

Place 8 slices of bread on the bottom of a 9" × 13" glass baking dish that has been coated with nonstick vegetable spray. Sprinkle the bread with 1½ cups of the cheese. Place the remaining bread slices over the cheese, then sprinkle the rest of the cheese on top. In a medium-sized bowl, whisk together the remaining ingredients. Pour over the bread and cheese, cover, and refrigerate for 2 hours or overnight. Preheat the oven to 350°F. and bake for 50 to 55 minutes or until puffy and golden and the center is set. Serve immediately.

NOTE: Cut or scoop into serving-sized portions.

Breakfast Crunch

4 cups

Wanna give your cereal an extra crunch? Or maybe liven up your yogurt? A sprinkle of this topping is guaranteed to wake up your taste buds, and the crunching noise might even wake up your entire family!

2 cups rolled oats (see Note)
⅔ cup flaked coconut
¾ cup mixed nuts, chopped
½ cup golden raisins
1½ tablespoons sesame seeds
⅔ cup firmly packed brown sugar, divided
⅔ cup water
⅔ cup sesame oil

Preheat the oven to 375°F. In a large bowl, mix together the rolled oats, coconut, nuts, raisins, sesame seeds, and half of the brown sugar. Place the water in a small bowl and whisk in the remaining brown sugar; add the oil and whisk again. Stir into the rolled oat mixture. Spread the mixture evenly over a large rimmed cookie sheet and bake for 30 to 35 minutes, mixing occasionally, until it browns evenly. Remove from the oven and allow to cool until it becomes crunchy, then store in an airtight container.

NOTE: Serve with yogurt, milk, or cereal, or use as a topping for frozen yogurt or ice cream. Oh, in case you're wondering about where to find rolled oats—it's uncooked regular oatmeal (not the quick-cooking type).

"Egg-cellent" Taco Brunch

12 servings

Tex-Mex flavors are as popular as ever, so why shouldn't we have Tex-Mex brunches, too? Yup, by simply replacing ground beef with scrambled eggs, we've got a brunch recipe that'll have your guests thanking you and Señor Food!

10 eggs
½ teaspoon salt
¼ teaspoon white pepper
2 tablespoons butter, divided
2 tablespoons dry taco seasoning mix
1 medium-sized onion, chopped (about 1 cup)
12 hard taco shells
1 medium-sized tomato, chopped (about 1 cup)
1 can (2.25 ounces) sliced black olives (½ cup)
1 cup (4 ounces) shredded Monterey Jack cheese

Preheat the oven to 400°F. In a large bowl, combine the eggs, salt, and pepper; beat well. In a large skillet, melt 1 tablespoon of the butter and cook the eggs until scrambled, but still moist. Remove to a bowl and stir in the taco seasoning; mix well. In the same skillet that you cooked the eggs in, melt the remaining butter and sauté the onion until tender and lightly browned. Stand the taco shells open end up in a 9" × 13" baking dish and divide the egg mixture evenly among the shells. Top each taco with equal amounts of onion, tomato, and olives. Top each taco with 2 tablespoons of the cheese and bake for 6 to 7 minutes or until the cheese is melted and bubbly.

NOTE: Top with taco sauce or salsa just before serving, if desired.

Cracker Omelet

6 to 8 servings

It's French toast—no, no, it's an omelet. . . . Well, you may not know this as an ordinary omelet, but the taste will grow on you. I promise you'll do more than "crack" a smile!

8 eggs
¼ cup milk
¼ teaspoon salt
¼ teaspoon pepper
4 ounces saltine crackers (¼ of a 1-pound box)
1 tablespoon butter

In a large bowl, whisk together the eggs, milk, salt, and pepper. Add the crackers and allow to soak for 3 to 4 minutes. In a large skillet, melt the butter over medium-high heat. Add the egg and cracker mixture and reduce the heat to medium. As the mixture begins to set, push it slightly toward the center so that the liquid runs to the edges of the skillet. Allow the omelet to cook for 5 to 6 minutes or until lightly browned on the bottom. Slide the omelet out of the pan onto a large plate. Invert the skillet over the omelet on the plate and turn the whole omelet over so that the uncooked side is face down in the skillet. (Be careful, the skillet will be hot.) Cook for 5 to 6 more minutes or until the center is set and the inside is firm.

NOTE: Serve with strawberry preserves or maple syrup.

Potato Frittata

6 to 8 servings

All the sleepy eyes in the house will open wide when they know you're serving up a batch of this favorite...

5 tablespoons butter
2 garlic cloves, minced
1 pound shredded frozen hash brown potatoes, thawed
5 eggs
⅓ cup water
½ teaspoon salt
½ teaspoon pepper
1 tablespoon dried chives

In a large nonstick skillet, melt the butter over medium-high heat and sauté the garlic for 10 to 15 seconds. Add the potatoes and continue cooking for about 10 minutes, using a plastic spatula to turn the potatoes occasionally until lightly browned. While the potatoes are cooking, in a medium-sized bowl, whisk together the eggs, water, salt, pepper, and chives. Add the egg mixture to the browned potatoes and reduce the heat to medium. As the mixture begins to set, push it slightly toward the center so that the liquid runs to the edges of the skillet. Reduce the heat to low and cover the skillet. Allow to cook for 11 to 12 minutes, then slide the omelet out of the pan onto a large plate. Invert the skillet over the frittata on the plate and turn the whole frittata over so that the uncooked side is face down in the skillet. (Be careful, the skillet will be hot.) Cook for 3 to 4 more minutes, until the bottom begins to brown, and serve immediately.

Upside-Down Noodle Wreath

12 to 14 servings

Yes, it's make-ahead easy. Yes, it's packed with flavor. Yes, it's perfect for brunch. And, of course, "OOH IT'S SO GOOD!!™"

½ cup firmly packed light brown sugar
16 maraschino cherries
¼ cup (½ stick) butter, melted
6 eggs
1 cup (½ pint) sour cream
¾ cup granulated sugar
1 teaspoon vanilla extract
½ teaspoon salt
1 can (20 ounces) crushed pineapple, well drained
1 package (16 ounces) fine egg noodles, cooked and drained

Preheat the oven to 350°F. Sprinkle the brown sugar into the bottom of a 10-inch Bundt pan that has been coated with nonstick vegetable spray. Place the cherries evenly on top of the brown sugar. Pour the melted butter evenly over the brown sugar and cherries; set aside. In a large bowl, with an electric beater, beat the eggs, sour cream, granulated sugar, vanilla, and salt until well blended. Stir in the crushed pineapple, then the drained noodles. Pour evenly into the Bundt pan and bake for 70 minutes or until the center is set and the top is lightly browned. Allow to cool for 20 minutes and invert gently onto a serving platter.

NOTE: Run a knife around the edges of the pan to help loosen it. And be careful when inverting it because it'll still be hot!

Pancake Muffin Surprises

1 dozen muffins

Who doesn't like surprises—especially when they're this good? It's worth making these just to watch the gang find the surprise in each muffin!

1¾ cups biscuit baking mix
¾ cup milk
2 eggs
½ cup maple or pancake syrup, plus extra for topping
2 medium-sized bananas, each cut into 6 pieces

Preheat the oven to 350°F. In a large bowl, combine the biscuit baking mix, milk, eggs, and ½ cup maple syrup. Pour about ¼ cup of the mixture into each cup of a 12-muffin tin that has been coated with nonstick vegetable spray. Place a piece of banana in the center of each. Bake for 20 to 25 minutes or until a wooden toothpick inserted in the center comes out clean. Serve with additional maple syrup for topping.

NOTE: You can make all of the muffins with bananas or another kind of fruit, or make them real surprises by using a few different kinds. I like to make a few with fresh banana, a few with canned pineapple chunks, and a few with canned mandarin orange slices for a big taste, a big easy, and a big surprise!

 Mr. Food®'s "take-along" suggestion

Hotel Rice Pudding

Recently I was at a hotel restaurant where they served a rice pudding that was incredible. I decided to do my own experimenting, and I came up with a version that tastes just as good—and I bet it's a lot easier!

¼ cup (½ stick) butter
½ cup sugar
4 eggs
½ teaspoon ground cinnamon
½ teaspoon salt
1 cup (½ pint) sour cream
1 cup raisins
⅓ cup chopped maraschino cherries
3 cups cooked long- or whole-grain rice (not instant)

Preheat the oven to 350°F. In a large bowl, cream the butter and sugar. With an electric beater, beat in the eggs one at a time. Add the remaining ingredients and mix well. Pour into a 1½-quart casserole dish that has been coated with nonstick vegetable spray and bake for 45 to 50 minutes or until the center is set.

NOTE: Most of the time, rice pudding is served cold, but this one tastes great right from the oven.

Potluck Favorites

I've got a little bit of everything in here for you—a little chicken, a little meat, and a little fish and pasta. When I think of these recipes, I think of back-door company. You know, good friends who you can be casual with and feel at home with. These aren't my fancy entertaining recipes; they're a terrific collection of "come on over" ones like Good Ol' Honey-Baked Chicken (page 66) and Mexican Lasagna Roll-ups (page 84). There's even All-in-One Dinner (page 76) that's meat loaf baked in a mashed potato crust. Now, don't they sound down-home inviting?

And just because these recipes are great for casual entertaining doesn't mean they aren't perfect for everyday family cooking, too. They're quick and easy—just what we need with today's hectic, fast-paced lifestyles. And what about serving them? Don't worry about getting out your fancy serving platters. Most of these can be served right out of the dish they're made in. Hooray! That means less cleanup! (And we all love that!)

So, go ahead—get out the trivets, put these right on the table, and watch everybody's eyes light up. You can sit back and enjoy dinner right along with the gang.

POTLUCK FAVORITES

Mr. Food®'s "take-along" suggestion

Honey Mustard Drumsticks

3 to 4 servings

You'll have them marching to the beat of a new drum once they get their fingers on these!

½ cup Dijon-style mustard
1½ teaspoons dry mustard
⅔ cup honey
⅓ cup light cream
1 tablespoon vegetable oil
8 chicken drumsticks (about 2 pounds)

In a small bowl, combine the mustards, honey, and cream; mix until smooth. In a medium-sized skillet, heat the oil over medium-high heat and add the chicken. Cook for 7 to 10 minutes, turning frequently. Reduce the heat to low and pour the mustard mixture over the chicken. Cover and simmer for 25 to 30 minutes, until the chicken is cooked through and the juices run clear. Arrange the chicken on a serving platter. Stir the sauce and pour over the chicken.

NOTE: Make sure you use 1½ teaspoons *dry* mustard (not prepared mustard) along with the Dijon mustard.

Oven-"Barbecued" Chicken

3 to 4 servings

No barbecues, no insects, no fuss! All the goodness of grilling...

1 cup ketchup
½ cup grape jelly
2 teaspoons dry mustard
1 cup raisins
1 teaspoon onion powder
¼ cup vegetable oil
1 chicken (2½ to 3 pounds), cut into 8 pieces

Preheat the oven to 350°F. In a medium-sized saucepan, combine the ketchup, jelly, mustard, raisins, and onion powder. Heat over low heat until the jelly is dissolved. Remove from the heat and set aside. In a large skillet, heat the oil over medium heat. Add the chicken and brown on all sides. Place the chicken in a roasting pan that has been coated with nonstick vegetable spray. Pour the sauce mixture over the chicken and cover with aluminum foil; bake for 45 minutes. Uncover and bake for 30 more minutes, until the chicken is cooked through and the juices run clear. Arrange chicken on a serving platter and pour the sauce on top. Serve the extra sauce alongside.

NOTE: Go ahead and use your fingers to eat this! And, of course, don't be afraid to dip your chicken again and again to use up all the extra sauce ... you wouldn't want to waste a drop.

Good Ol' Honey-Baked Chicken

3 to 4 servings

Always looking for a new way to make chicken? Well, here's an old Southern favorite made a new way—with the sweetness of honey and the tang of paprika and mustard.

¾ cup honey
1 chicken (2½ to 3 pounds), cut into 8 pieces
1¼ cups biscuit baking mix
2 teaspoons dry mustard
½ teaspoon paprika
1 teaspoon salt
½ teaspoon pepper
Nonstick vegetable spray

Preheat the oven to 350°F. Place the honey in a shallow bowl; coat the chicken with the honey and set aside. Combine the remaining ingredients (except the spray) in a shallow pie plate; dredge the chicken in the mixture. Place the chicken on a large rimmed cookie sheet that has been coated with nonstick vegetable spray. Coat the chicken generously with additional nonstick vegetable spray and bake for 60 to 75 minutes, until brown and the juices run clear.

Mr. Food®'s "take-along" suggestion

Chicken Rice Pie

6 to 8 servings

So good, one serving is never enough!

1 package (6.9 ounces) chicken-flavored rice and pasta mix
¼ cup vegetable oil
2 pounds boneless, skinless chicken breasts or thighs,
cut into 1-inch chunks
2 large zucchini, sliced lengthwise, then cut into ¼-inch slices
3 medium-sized carrots, peeled and sliced lengthwise,
then cut into ⅛-inch slices
2 cans (14½ ounces each) stewed tomatoes,
drained with liquid reserved
2 teaspoons salt
1 teaspoon pepper
2 tablespoons cornstarch

Preheat the oven to 350°F. Prepare the rice and pasta mix according to the package directions. Meanwhile, heat the oil in a large saucepan. Sauté the chicken, zucchini, and carrots for 5 to 7 minutes over medium-high heat. Add the drained tomatoes, salt, and pepper; mix well. Combine the cornstarch and the reserved tomato liquid; mix until smooth. Pour the cornstarch mixture into the saucepan and heat for 1 to 2 minutes, until slightly thickened. Place the chicken mixture into a 2½-quart casserole dish that has been coated with nonstick vegetable spray. When the rice mixture is finished cooking, spread over the top of the chicken mixture. Bake for 1 hour or until heated through.

NOTE: You can prepare this in advance and keep it in the refrigerator until you are ready to bake it. And, by the way, you can find the rice and pasta mix in the supermarket rice section.

Nothing-to-It Chicken

3 to 4 servings

What could be easier? It's so good it leaves them wanting more!

½ cup creamy Parmesan salad dressing
⅓ cup chicken broth
2 teaspoons Dijon-style mustard
½ teaspoon salt
½ teaspoon pepper
1 chicken (2½ to 3 pounds), cut into 8 pieces

Preheat the oven to 350°F. In a large bowl, combine all of the ingredients except the chicken; mix well. Add the chicken pieces and coat well. Place the chicken in a 9" × 13" baking dish and pour the remaining mixture over the top. Bake for 1 hour or until the juices run clear.

NOTE: Want all dark-meat chicken? Go ahead. Or maybe all white meat? Make it your own way.

Spicy Corn Bread Chicken

3 to 4 servings

Two great tastes rolled into one!

1 cup buttermilk
1 cup yellow cornmeal
½ teaspoon salt
¼ teaspoon pepper
1 tablespoon chili powder
2 teaspoons onion powder
2 teaspoons garlic powder
8 chicken drumsticks
Nonstick vegetable spray

Preheat the oven to 350°F. Place the buttermilk in a shallow bowl. In another bowl, combine the remaining ingredients except the drumsticks and the spray; mix well. Dip the drumsticks into the buttermilk and then into the cornmeal mixture, completely coating the drumsticks. Place in a single layer in a 9" × 13" baking dish that has been coated with nonstick vegetable spray. Coat the drumsticks with additional nonstick vegetable spray and bake for 50 to 55 minutes, until browned and the juices run clear.

NOTE: Hot or cold, boy, these are good!

Spicy Spud Chicken

3 to 4 servings

Perfect for the buffet table or the picnic basket—but the best part is the taste.... Mmm!

⅓ cup butter, melted
⅔ cup instant mashed potato flakes
3 tablespoons dry taco seasoning mix
⅛ teaspoon cayenne pepper
⅓ cup grated Parmesan cheese
1 chicken (2½ to 3 pounds), cut into 8 pieces

Preheat the oven to 375°F. Place the melted butter in a shallow dish. In a large bowl, combine the remaining ingredients except the chicken. Dip the chicken pieces into the butter, then the potato mixture, coating well. Place in a 9" × 13" baking dish that has been coated with nonstick vegetable spray and bake for 45 to 60 minutes or until the breading is browned and the chicken juices run clear.

Easy Dinner Pie

6 servings

Pie for dinner? Yes, sir! I mean a pie made of chicken and mashed potatoes. Go ahead, have a wedge or two tonight.

1 pound fresh ground chicken
1 teaspoon dried dill
1 teaspoon salt
½ teaspoon white pepper
2 cups seasoned mashed potatoes (see Note)
½ teaspoon paprika

Preheat the oven to 350°F. In a large bowl, combine the chicken, dill, salt, and pepper; mix well. Form a ring of the chicken mixture around the edge of a 9-inch deep-dish pie plate. Place the cooked mashed potatoes in the center of the chicken ring. Sprinkle the paprika over the potatoes and bake for 30 to 35 minutes or until the chicken is completely cooked. Cut into serving-sized wedges and serve hot.

NOTE: Smashed Potatoes (page 139) are perfect in this recipe. They add great color and flavor.

Make-Ahead Chicken

3 to 4 servings

No precooking the pasta, no complicated directions, and no leftovers 'cause it's so good nobody will leave till it's all gone! You'll see.

2 cups cooked chicken, cut into ½-inch cubes
1 package (9 ounces) frozen mixed vegetables, thawed and drained
8 ounces (2 cups) uncooked elbow macaroni
1 cup (4 ounces) shredded Cheddar cheese
1 can (10¾ ounces) cream of mushroom soup
2 cups water
1 cup milk
½ teaspoon curry powder
1 cup cornflake crumbs
3 tablespoons butter, melted

In a large bowl, combine all the ingredients except the cornflake crumbs and butter; mix well. Place in an 8-inch square baking dish that has been coated with nonstick vegetable spray and cover tightly with aluminum foil. Refrigerate for 6 to 8 hours, or overnight. About an hour before serving time, preheat the oven to 350°F. In a small bowl, combine the cornflake crumbs and butter; mix well. Stir the chicken mixture, then sprinkle the crumb topping evenly over the top. Bake for 45 to 50 minutes, until golden brown.

NOTE: If you don't care for the flavor of curry, try an equal amount of dried basil for an Italian treat, or dried dill for that "right from the garden" taste.

Crowd-Pleasing Brisket

10 to 12 servings

Everybody's favorite condiments—ketchup and mustard—make this brisket a sure crowd-pleaser.

One 4- to 4½-pound fresh brisket of beef
2½ cups ketchup
¾ cup prepared mustard
1 cup firmly packed brown sugar
½ cup water

Preheat the oven to 350°F. Place the brisket in a large roasting pan that has been coated with nonstick vegetable spray. In a large bowl, combine the ketchup, mustard, and brown sugar. Remove 1 cup of this sauce to a medium-sized bowl and add the water to it; mix well and pour around the meat in the pan. Pour the remainder of the sauce over the top of the meat, making sure that some of it stays on top. Cover tightly with aluminum foil and bake for 3 to 3½ hours or until the meat is fork-tender. Slice across the grain and serve with sauce over the top.

NOTE: To make your whole meal a crowd-pleaser, serve this with Smashed Potatoes (page 139) and Creamed Spinach (page 152).

All-in-One Dinner

6 servings

*Meat loaf, potatoes, and veggies all wrapped up in one dynamite dinner...
Now that's smart cooking!*

1½ pounds ground beef
1 can (10½ ounces) condensed vegetarian vegetable soup
1 cup dry bread crumbs
½ teaspoon salt
½ teaspoon pepper
½ teaspoon onion powder
3 lightly beaten eggs, used separately
2 cups warm seasoned mashed potatoes

Preheat the oven to 350°F. In a large bowl, mix together all the ingredients except the potatoes and 1 egg. On a rimmed cookie sheet or in a 9" × 13" glass baking dish that has been coated with non-stick vegetable spray, form the mixture into an oval-shaped loaf and bake for 1 hour. While whipping the mashed potatoes with a fork, add the remaining beaten egg and whip until well blended. When the meat loaf has cooked for 1 hour, remove from the oven and drain off the grease in the pan. Completely "frost" the meat loaf with the potatoes and return to the oven for 15 to 20 minutes or until the potatoes are slightly crusted and heated through.

  Mr. Food®'s "take-along" suggestion

Make-Ahead Fajitas

10 fajitas

While you're waiting for the gang to return from the game, you can make these and pop them in the oven. When they get home, boy, will they be surprised!

3 tablespoons vegetable oil, divided
2 large onions, cut into 8 wedges each
1 large green bell pepper, seeded and cut into ½-inch strips
1 large red bell pepper, seeded and cut into ½-inch strips
1 pound flank steak, cut into thin strips
2 tablespoons dry fajita seasoning
Ten 7-inch flour tortillas
1 cup (4 ounces) shredded Cheddar cheese
1 cup (½ pint) sour cream
1 cup salsa

Preheat the oven to 350°F. In a large skillet, heat 2 tablespoons of the oil over medium-high heat. Add the onions and peppers and sauté for 10 to 12 minutes or until the onions are lightly browned; place in a large bowl and set aside. Heat the remaining 1 tablespoon of oil in the same skillet and add the flank steak. Add the fajita seasoning and sauté for 3 to 4 minutes, until the steak begins to brown. Return the vegetables to the skillet and cook for 3 to 4 more minutes, stirring occasionally. Divide the flank steak mixture equally among the tortillas and roll up. Place the roll-ups seam sides down in a 9" × 13" baking dish that has been coated with nonstick vegetable spray. Sprinkle with cheese, loosely cover with aluminum foil, and bake for 15 to 20 minutes. Serve with sour cream and salsa.

NOTE: You can make these ahead of time. Just cover and refrigerate them after filling and rolling them. Then bake for 20 to 25 minutes at 350°F. before serving.

South-of-the-Border Beef

8 to 10 servings

A viewer wrote to me with this family favorite.... I bet it'll be a favorite of your family soon.

½ teaspoon garlic powder
½ teaspoon onion powder
½ teaspoon black pepper
⅛ teaspoon cayenne pepper
½ cup bottled steak sauce
One 4-pound rump roast
1 medium-sized onion, thinly sliced

Preheat the oven to 350°F. In a small bowl, combine the garlic powder, onion powder, black and cayenne peppers, and the steak sauce. Place the roast in a roasting pan and brush the sauce mixture generously over the roast. Place the sliced onions on top and bake for 1¾ to 2 hours or until desired doneness. Cut across the grain.

NOTE: Have some leftover roast on rye bread for really great sandwiches.

Caramelized Corned Beef

12 to 15 servings

Hosting a party and looking for just the right dish to be the focal point of the meal? This one will do it—'cause it could be your edible centerpiece!

One 4- to 4½-pound cooked corned beef
½ cup apricot preserves
2 tablespoons brown sugar
1 tablespoon soy sauce

Preheat the oven to 350°F. Place the corned beef in a large roasting pan that has been coated with nonstick vegetable spray. In a small bowl, combine the remaining ingredients. Spread evenly over the corned beef. Cover tightly with aluminum foil and bake for 2 to 2½ hours, until the corned beef is fork-tender. Baste with the glazing juices several times during cooking and uncover for the final 20 minutes.

NOTE: Slice this thick for dinners or thin for sandwiches and appetizers.

Pot Roast Cacciatore

8 to 10 servings

You know that rich cacciatore sauce that's usually served with chicken? Well, here we get to combine those great flavors with our old standby—pot roast. Your company may never want to leave!

One 3½- to 4-pound bottom round roast
1 red bell pepper, seeded and cut into ½-inch strips
1 green bell pepper, seeded and cut into ½-inch strips
3 small onions, quartered and onion segments separated
1 package (10 ounces) fresh mushrooms, sliced
1 jar (25 to 28 ounces) spaghetti sauce
¼ cup water
¼ cup dry red or white wine
3 garlic cloves, chopped
½ teaspoon dried basil
¼ teaspoon salt
¼ teaspoon pepper

Preheat the oven to 350°F. Place the roast in a 9" × 13" baking dish that has been coated with nonstick vegetable spray. Place the peppers, onions, and mushrooms around the roast. In a medium-sized bowl, combine the remaining ingredients. Pour the sauce over the roast and vegetables. Cover tightly with aluminum foil and roast for 3 to 3½ hours or until the center of the meat is fork-tender. Slice the meat across the grain in ¼-inch slices and place it back into the baking dish; return it to the pan to cook for 5 more minutes. Serve with the sauce and vegetables.

NOTE: Make this and slice it a day in advance, then when company comes, just cover and heat it, and your main dish is ready in minutes.

Banquet Brisket

10 to 12 servings

It doesn't matter what the get-together is called—a buffet, a celebration, a party—this entrée should be on the guest list.

One 4- to 4½-pound fresh brisket of beef
1 pound fresh whole mushrooms, cleaned and halved
3 small onions, quartered
10 garlic cloves
1 can (6 ounces) tomato paste
2 cups water
2½ teaspoons salt
¾ teaspoon pepper
1 bay leaf

Preheat the oven to 350°F. Place the brisket in a large roasting pan that has been coated with nonstick vegetable spray; set aside. In a large food processor or blender, on high speed, purée the mushrooms, onions, garlic, tomato paste, water, salt, and pepper. Pour the mixture over the meat. Place the bay leaf into the sauce in the pan. Cover tightly with aluminum foil and cook for 3 to 3½ hours or until the brisket is fork-tender. When the brisket is completely cooked, slice it across the grain; return it to the pan and cook for 5 more minutes. **Be sure to remove the bay leaf before serving.**

NOTE: Serve this with the pan juices.

Mexican Lasagna Roll-ups

8 servings

This is cross-cultural cooking at its best—Mexican, Italian, American . . . And all the tastes come through with a big thumbs up!

8 uncooked lasagna noodles
3 cups salsa, divided
1 pound ground beef
1 package (1¼ ounces) dry taco seasoning mix
1 cup (4 ounces) shredded Monterey Jack cheese
1 cup (½ pint) sour cream
1 can (2.25 ounces) sliced black olives, drained (½ cup)

Preheat the oven to 350°F. Cook the lasagna noodles according to the package directions; drain and set aside. Spread 1 cup of the salsa onto the bottom of a 9" × 13" baking dish that has been coated with nonstick vegetable spray; set aside. In a medium-sized skillet, brown the ground beef over medium-high heat for about 10 minutes; drain excess liquid. Stir in the taco seasoning mix and 1 cup of the salsa. Cut each noodle in half, spread each half with 2 tablespoons of the beef mixture, and roll up. Place the lasagna roll-ups in the baking dish. Pour the remaining cup of salsa over the roll-ups and sprinkle the top with the cheese. Cover loosely with aluminum foil and bake for 22 to 25 minutes or until the cheese is melted. Before serving, spoon 1 tablespoon of sour cream on each roll-up and sprinkle with sliced black olives.

NOTE: Mild, medium, or hot salsa . . . the choice is yours.

Veal Loaf Florentine

6 to 8 servings

Who could forget the days of TV dinners and that all-time favorite—meat loaf? Well, here's an updated meat loaf made with veal and spinach that'll make your guests remember the good ol' days... and know they're even better today.

1½ pounds ground veal
1 package (9 ounces) frozen creamed spinach, thawed
2 eggs
1 cup dry bread crumbs
½ teaspoon garlic powder
1 teaspoon salt
½ teaspoon pepper

Preheat the oven to 350°F. In a large bowl, combine all of the ingredients; mix well. Form into a loaf on a large rimmed cookie sheet. Bake for 55 to 60 minutes or until the meat is cooked through.

NOTE: For a nice surprise, place some hard-boiled eggs in the loaf by forming the loaf around the eggs. When you slice the baked loaf . . . watch their faces!

Finger Lickin' Spareribs

5 to 6 servings

These are perfect for back-door company, since you're gonna want to eat these ribs with your hands!

5 pounds pork spareribs
½ cup vegetable oil
½ cup soy sauce
2 tablespoons molasses
¼ cup firmly packed brown sugar
2 teaspoons ground ginger
2 teaspoons dry mustard
2 teaspoons garlic powder
2 teaspoons seasoned salt

Place the spareribs in a large pot and add just enough water to cover them; boil the ribs over medium-high heat for 30 minutes or until fork-tender. Preheat the oven to 375°F. In a small bowl, combine the remaining ingredients; mix well. Place the ribs in a large roasting pan and baste heavily with the sauce. Bake for 30 minutes, basting occasionally and turning once after 15 minutes. Remove the ribs from the pan and cut them apart every 2 to 3 ribs for easier eating. Serve with the remaining sauce.

NOTE: Why not make this part of a platter that includes Chinese Doubles Dippers (page 15) and Creamy Crab Wontons (page 17)?

Killer Kielbasa Chili

4 to 6 servings

Take a traditional favorite—chili—and spice it up with Polish kielbasa to make it killer delicious.

1 pound ground beef
1 large onion, coarsely chopped (about 1½ cups)
2 teaspoons chili powder
2 teaspoons ground cumin
8 ounces kielbasa, sliced in half lengthwise,
then into ¼-inch pieces
1 can (16 ounces) red kidney beans, drained
1 jar (8 ounces) medium picante sauce
1 cup vegetable juice
1 can (8 ounces) tomato sauce

In a large saucepan, brown the ground beef; drain excess liquid. Add the onion and sauté for 4 to 5 minutes, until the onion is soft. Add the remaining ingredients and bring to a boil. Reduce the heat to low and simmer for 20 minutes, stirring occasionally.

NOTE: To really spice up this "killer" chili, use hot picante sauce.

Mexican Fish Fillets

5 to 6 servings

The last time I went to a Mexican restaurant I tried some fish and, boy, it was super! I made my own shortcut version and it's fantástico!

2 pounds white-fleshed fish fillets (like whiting, haddock,
or cod), thawed if frozen
3 cups salsa, well drained
¼ cup sour cream
1 can (2.25 ounces) sliced black olives, drained (½ cup)
⅔ cup (about 2½ ounces) shredded Monterey Jack cheese

Preheat the oven to 400°F. Place the fish fillets on a large rimmed cookie sheet that has been coated with nonstick vegetable spray and bake for 20 minutes. Combine the salsa, sour cream, and olives in a medium-sized bowl; mix well. After the fillets are cooked, remove them from the oven. Spoon ¼ cup of the salsa mixture over each fillet and top with the cheese. Bake for 4 to 5 more minutes, or until the cheese is melted. Serve immediately.

NOTE: For a spicy fish dish, add some sliced jalapeño peppers along with the sliced olives.

Potato Chip Fish Fillets

4 to 6 servings

When you don't have time to deep-fry your fish, here's a quick and easy way to make that same crispy, crunchy fish in your oven.

2 cups crushed plain potato chips
1 teaspoon dried parsley flakes
½ teaspoon white pepper
½ teaspoon onion powder
¼ cup (½ stick) butter, melted
1 to 1½ pounds white-fleshed fish fillets (like whiting,
haddock, or cod), thawed if frozen

Preheat the oven to 400°F. In a shallow dish, combine the crushed potato chips, parsley, pepper, and onion powder. Brush both sides of the fillets with the melted butter, then coat with the potato chip mixture. Place on a large rimmed cookie sheet that has been coated with nonstick vegetable spray and bake for 20 to 22 minutes or until golden brown.

NOTE: You can substitute 1 tablespoon chopped fresh parsley for the dried parsley flakes.

Seafood Lasagna

8 to 10 servings

Nobody ever said that lasagna had to be made with ground beef or even spinach. So why not enjoy your pasta shells overflowing with shrimp and crab for that fresh-from-the-seas flavor?

1 pound uncooked medium-sized pasta shells
6 tablespoons (¾ stick) butter
6 tablespoons all-purpose flour
3 cups milk
½ teaspoon salt
½ teaspoon white pepper
1½ cups (6 ounces) shredded Swiss cheese
1 can (14½ ounces) stewed tomatoes
12 ounces medium-sized shrimp, cooked, peeled, and deveined
1 package (10 ounces) imitation crabmeat, flaked

Preheat the oven to 350°F. Cook the shells according to the package directions; drain and set aside in a large bowl. In a large saucepan, melt the butter over medium heat and slowly add the flour, stirring until the flour is well blended. Add the milk gradually and stir until blended. Add the salt and pepper and stir the sauce constantly until thickened. Add the cheese and stir until melted. Pour the cheese sauce and remaining ingredients over the shells; mix well. Pour into a 9" × 13" baking dish that has been coated with nonstick vegetable spray and bake for 30 minutes until hot and bubbly.

Potluck Ziti

6 to 8 servings

Don't hurry—in less than an hour you can have this new version of a tuna and cheese casserole ready to receive raves from your guests . . . and your family, too!

8 ounces uncooked ziti, penne, or other tubular pasta
2 tablespoons butter
1 small onion, chopped (about ½ cup)
½ cup chopped red bell pepper
1 can (10¾ ounces) cream of mushroom soup
1 container (15 ounces) ricotta cheese
2 cans (6½ ounces each) solid white tuna, drained and flaked
2 cups (8 ounces) shredded mozzarella cheese, divided

Preheat the oven to 350°F. In a large pot of boiling salted water, cook the pasta according to the package directions; drain, rinse with cold water, drain again, and set aside in a large bowl. In a medium-sized skillet, melt the butter over medium heat and sauté the onion and red bell pepper until tender, about 4 minutes. Add to the pasta along with the mushroom soup, ricotta, tuna, and 1 cup of the mozzarella cheese; mix well. Pour the mixture into a 2½-quart baking dish that has been coated with nonstick vegetable spray. Top with the remaining mozzarella cheese and bake for 30 minutes.

NOTE: Why not make this ahead and freeze it? Then all you have to do is thaw, heat, and serve.

Baked Ziti with Sausage and Artichokes

6 to 8 servings

It's fancy enough for company, yet simple enough to be a potluck favorite any night of the week.

1 pound uncooked ziti
1 pound mild Italian sausage, casings removed
2 cans (14 ounces each) quartered artichoke hearts, drained
1 jar (25 to 28 ounces) spaghetti sauce
1 can (28 ounces) crushed tomatoes, undrained
½ teaspoon garlic powder
½ teaspoon pepper
4 cups (1 pound) shredded mozzarella cheese, divided

Preheat the oven to 350°F. In a large pot of boiling salted water, cook the pasta according to the package directions; drain, rinse with cold water, drain again, and set aside in a large bowl. In a large skillet, sauté the sausage over medium-high heat for 5 to 6 minutes or until no pink remains, breaking it up as it cooks. Drain the liquid from the cooked sausage and add it to the ziti along with the artichoke hearts, spaghetti sauce, crushed tomatoes, garlic powder, pepper, and 3 cups of the mozzarella cheese; mix well. Pour into a 9" × 13" baking dish that has been coated with nonstick vegetable spray and sprinkle the remaining 1 cup of cheese over the top. Cover tightly with aluminum foil and bake for 1 to 1½ hours or until heated through.

NOTE: You can buy canned artichokes already quartered, or buy whole canned ones and cut them yourself.

Ravioli Pesto Pie

3 to 4 servings

Part ravioli, part pizza, part casserole—it's all pie! And it's like an Italian buffet in one dish.

1 bag (20 ounces) frozen cheese ravioli
½ cup (4 ounces) pesto sauce
1 jar (2 ounces) chopped pimientos
¼ cup grated Parmesan cheese
1.5 ounces sliced pepperoni (about 25 slices)
½ cup (2 ounces) shredded mozzarella cheese

Preheat the oven to 350°F. Boil the ravioli according to the package directions; drain. In a large bowl, combine the pesto, pimientos, Parmesan cheese, and pepperoni slices. Add the ravioli and toss until evenly coated. Place in a 9-inch deep-dish pie plate and top with the mozzarella cheese. Cover loosely with aluminum foil and bake for 20 to 25 minutes or until the cheese is melted and the ravioli is heated through.

NOTE: Go ahead and use your favorite ravioli. They can be filled with meat, mushrooms, or even pesto.

Minestrone Casserole

6 to 8 servings

It's not a soup, it's a casserole! It's so thick and hearty that you'll probably need a fork and a spoon to eat it!

1 pound bulk Italian sausage
½ cup chopped celery (1 stalk)
6 ounces (2 cups) uncooked medium-sized pasta shells
2 cans (14½ ounces each) whole tomatoes, chopped
1 can (15 ounces) kidney beans, undrained
1 package (10 ounces) frozen whole kernel corn,
thawed and drained
1 teaspoon dried thyme leaves
1 teaspoon garlic powder

Preheat the oven to 375°F. In a medium-sized skillet, brown the sausage and celery over medium-high heat for 8 to 10 minutes; drain excess liquid. Pour the sausage and celery mixture into a large bowl and add the remaining ingredients; mix well. Pour into a 2½-quart casserole dish that has been coated with nonstick vegetable spray; cover and bake for 50 minutes or until heated through and the pasta is cooked.

NOTE: Serve with State Fair Herb Bread (page 199) and you'll have a perfect rainy day meal.

Bow Tie Lasagna

8 to 10 servings

Bow ties are a must at fancy functions, but this time they're pasta bow ties that you need. And the results are a real party pleaser.

1 package (12 ounces) uncooked bow tie pasta
1 container (15 ounces) ricotta cheese
1 package (10 ounces) frozen chopped broccoli,
thawed and drained
1 jar (25 to 28 ounces) spaghetti sauce, divided
1 jar (12 ounces) mild picante sauce
½ teaspoon garlic powder
½ teaspoon salt
2 cups (8 ounces) shredded mozzarella cheese

Preheat the oven to 350°F. In a large pot of boiling salted water, cook the pasta according to the package directions; drain, rinse with cold water, drain again, and set aside. Meanwhile, in a medium-sized bowl, combine the ricotta and broccoli; set aside. In another medium-sized bowl, combine the spaghetti sauce, picante sauce, garlic powder, and salt. Spread 1 cup of the spaghetti sauce mixture on the bottom of a 9" × 13" baking dish that has been coated with nonstick vegetable spray. Layer half of the cooked pasta evenly over the sauce. Using a tablespoon, evenly cover the pasta with the ricotta mixture. Cover with the remaining pasta, followed by the remaining spaghetti sauce mixture. Top with the mozzarella cheese and bake for 35 to 40 minutes, until the cheese is melted and golden.

NOTE: Don't worry if you don't have any bow tie pasta on hand. You can surely use spirals and elbows or another favorite.

Fettuccine Primavera

6 to 8 servings

Fettuccine Primavera is normally made at the last minute, but you can make this one in advance so that you have time to visit with your gang when they arrive.

1 pound uncooked fettuccine
2 cups chopped zucchini (1 large zucchini)
1 medium-sized red bell pepper, chopped (about 1 cup)
1 cup sliced mushrooms
2 cans (10¾ ounces each) condensed cream of mushroom soup
1 can (10½ ounces) condensed chicken broth
1½ cups milk
1 teaspoon garlic powder
½ teaspoon black pepper
2½ cups grated Parmesan cheese
1 can (2.8 ounces) French-fried onions

Preheat the oven to 350°F. In a large pot of boiling salted water, cook the fettuccine according to the package directions; drain, rinse with cold water, drain again, and set aside. In a medium-sized bowl, combine the chopped zucchini, red pepper, and mushrooms; set aside. In a large bowl, combine the remaining ingredients except the French-fried onions. Add the vegetables and the fettuccine, tossing until evenly coated. Place in a 9" × 13" baking dish that has been coated with nonstick vegetable spray and sprinkle with the French-fried onions. Cover with aluminum foil and bake for 45 to 50 minutes or until heated through.

NOTE: Add your favorite fresh or frozen (thawed and drained) veggies.

Inviting Main Courses

Sometimes you need something a little special to serve for important occasions. You want something quick and easy to put together that'll make your guests think you spent all day in the kitchen preparing!

This chapter has recipes that are perfect for making that special happening come off just right. Try serving Creamy Basil Pork Chops (page 126) or Angelic Seafood (page 131). Those are sure ways to get your favorite company to stay a little longer! For a holiday celebration why not treat everyone to Garlic Roast (page 118) or Cornish Hens with Apricot Stuffing (page 101)? They're all super!

Don't forget to make your table look special, too. Be sure to read my Party Planning Tips at the front of the book (page xvii). Those pages give you suggestions for setting your table and fancying up individual plates and serving dishes with simple garnishes (page xxii) that'll make your family and guests feel like royalty. And that's just what we *should* do every once in a while—let people know they're special!

INVITING MAIN COURSES

Mr. Food®'s "take-along" suggestion

Mr. Food®'s "take-along" suggestion

Cornish Hens with Apricot Stuffing

6 servings

Cornish hens always look so holiday special. This is one easy dish that'll make your guests feel pampered.

3 cups apricot nectar, divided
3 tablespoons butter
3 cups one-step stuffing mix
3 tablespoons chopped almonds
Six 1-pound Cornish hens
1 tablespoon poultry seasoning
1½ teaspoons salt
2 tablespoons vegetable oil

Preheat the oven to 350°F. In a medium-sized saucepan, combine 1½ cups of nectar and the butter and bring to a boil over medium heat. Remove from the heat and stir in the stuffing mix and almonds, cover, and allow to sit for 5 minutes. Prepare the hens by removing (and discarding) the insides and rinsing them inside and out with cold water. Pat dry and stuff each hen with ½ cup of the stuffing mixture. In a small bowl or cup, combine the poultry seasoning, salt, and oil and rub each hen all over with the mixture. Place the remaining 1½ cups of nectar in the bottom of a large roasting pan that has been coated with nonstick vegetable spray and place the hens in the nectar. Bake for 30 minutes, then baste with the nectar. Bake for 40 to 45 more minutes or until completely cooked and golden brown.

NOTE: Make sure that you cook the hens right after stuffing them.

Celebration Chicken

3 to 4 servings

Some people need a reason to celebrate—and there are lots of reasons, not just birthdays and anniversaries but promotions, raises, and lottery winnings (we hope!). And there's no better way to celebrate than with good food!

2 tablespoons vegetable oil
1 chicken (2½ to 3 pounds), cut into 8 pieces
1 medium-sized onion, chopped (about 1 cup)
1½ teaspoons curry powder
1 teaspoon salt
1 can (16 ounces) peaches in heavy syrup, drained, chopped, and ⅔ cup juice reserved

Place the vegetable oil in a large skillet and heat over medium-high heat. Cook the chicken for about 10 minutes, turning occasionally, until browned. Drain the oil from the pan. Add the remaining ingredients (including the reserved peach syrup); mix well. Reduce the heat to medium-low, cover, and simmer for 25 to 30 minutes, turning the chicken occasionally, until cooked through.

NOTE: Plan on making steamed rice with this because you won't want to miss any of the yummy juices.

Apricot Mango Chicken

6 servings

Be careful not to tell anyone that you're planning to serve this to company, 'cause they'll tell somebody, who'll tell somebody else, and before you know it, the whole neighborhood will be lined up at your door!

6 boneless, skinless chicken breast halves (1½ to 1¾ pounds)
½ teaspoon salt, divided
1 can (16 ounces) apricot halves, drained
1 tablespoon brown sugar
¼ teaspoon cayenne pepper
1 ripe mango, peeled, pitted, and diced

Preheat the broiler. Place the chicken breasts flat on a large rimmed cookie sheet that has been coated with nonstick vegetable spray. Sprinkle with ¼ teaspoon of the salt and broil for 12 to 15 minutes. Meanwhile, in a blender, combine the remaining ingredients except the mango and blend on medium speed until a chunky purée forms. In a small bowl, combine the diced mango and the purée. Spoon the mixture over the top of the chicken and broil for 8 to 10 more minutes, until the chicken is done and no pink remains.

NOTE: Mangoes are available almost year-round now in your supermarket produce department, but if you can't get one, you can substitute two fresh peaches here and it'll still be a hit.

"Drunken" Chicken

4 servings

This is like one of those fancy tropical drinks—you know, the ones with the rum, lime juice, and cream—but baked on top of chicken, it'll really impress your company. Oh . . . made this way, you don't need a straw.

4 boneless, skinless chicken breast halves (1 to 1¼ pounds),
flattened to ½-inch thickness
2 tablespoons butter
1 can (4 ounces) sliced mushrooms, drained
1 cup (½ pint) sour cream

Marinade
¼ cup light rum
¼ teaspoon ground nutmeg
1 tablespoon soy sauce
1 tablespoon lime juice
1 tablespoon brown sugar
¼ teaspoon crushed red pepper
⅛ teaspoon ground ginger

Place the chicken in a 7" × 11" glass baking dish in a single layer; set aside. In a small bowl, combine the marinade ingredients. Mix well and pour over the chicken. Cover the chicken and refrigerate for 30 minutes, turning once. Then melt the butter in a large skillet over medium heat. Remove the chicken from the marinade, reserving excess marinade, and sauté the chicken for 7 to 9 minutes, until cooked through and golden. Remove the chicken to a serving platter and keep warm. Add the mushrooms and reserved marinade to the skillet and heat for 1 to 2 minutes. Gradually add the sour cream, stirring to blend. Cook the sauce over low heat for 5 to 10 minutes, until slightly thickened. Serve the sauce over the chicken breasts. Sprinkle with additional nutmeg, if desired.

Sunshine Chicken

6 to 8 servings

Don't we all feel better when the sun shines? I sure do. This recipe helps us bring that good feeling to the dinner table.

2 chickens (2½ to 3 pounds each), each cut into 8 pieces
1 teaspoon salt
½ teaspoon white pepper
2 cans (10¾ ounces each) Cheddar cheese soup
1¼ cups dry white wine
1 tablespoon dried parsley flakes or 2 tablespoons fresh chopped parsley

Preheat the oven to 350°F. Place the chicken pieces in two 9" × 13" baking dishes that have been coated with nonstick vegetable spray. Rub the chicken evenly with the salt and pepper. Bake, uncovered, for 45 minutes. Then, in a medium-sized bowl, whisk together the soup, wine, and parsley. Drain the liquid from the chicken; pour the sauce mixture over the chicken and return it to the oven for 15 to 20 minutes, or until the chicken is completely cooked through.

NOTE: You can easily cut this recipe in half if you're only expecting a small group for dinner.

Holiday Stuffed Capon

6 to 8 servings

It doesn't have to be Thanksgiving or Christmas to have this fancy-looking stuffed favorite on your table. In fact, this one is so easy, I wouldn't be surprised if your family sees that holiday look more often.

Cornbread Stuffing
1¼ cups water
¼ cup (½ stick) butter
1 package (8 ounces) cornbread stuffing cubes
3 ounces pitted dates, chopped (about 12 dates)
2 tablespoons chopped pecans
3 tablespoons mayonnaise
1 tablespoon sour cream
½ teaspoon ground cumin
½ teaspoon ground ginger
½ teaspoon ground dried thyme
½ teaspoon salt
½ teaspoon white pepper
One 7- to 8-pound capon

Place the water and butter in a medium-sized saucepan and bring to a boil over high heat. Add the cornbread stuffing mix and remove from the heat. Toss lightly until the stuffing mix is thoroughly moistened. Let sit for 5 minutes, then add the chopped dates and pecans. Toss lightly and set aside to cool. In a medium-sized bowl, combine the remaining ingredients except the capon; set aside ¼ cup of the

    Mr. Food®'s "take-along" suggestion

mixture. Loosen the skin from the breast and thighs of the capon and rub the mayonnaise mixture under the skin, inside the cavity, and on the exterior of the chicken, coating well. Stuff the chicken with the cornbread stuffing. Tie the legs together and place on a rack in a medium-sized roasting pan that has been coated with non-stick vegetable spray. Bake the capon for 1½ to 2 hours or until golden brown and the juices run clear, basting occasionally with the reserved mayonnaise mixture and the pan drippings.

NOTE: If you prefer, you can use your own favorite flavor stuffing cubes in place of the cornbread cubes. There are no rules!

Chinese Almond Noodle Chicken

4 to 6 servings

As soon as your neighbors ring your doorbell, they'll be wondering what smells so good. I doubt you'll have to ring a dinner bell to get them to the table!

1 can (3 ounces) chow mein noodles
½ cup blanched almonds
½ teaspoon garlic powder
½ teaspoon salt
½ teaspoon pepper
2 eggs
1 tablespoon soy sauce
5 to 6 boneless, skinless chicken breast halves
(1¼ to 1½ pounds)

Preheat the oven to 350°F. In a food processor, process the noodles, almonds, garlic powder, salt, and pepper until the noodles and almonds are finely crushed; transfer to a shallow pan or bowl. In another small bowl, beat together the eggs and soy sauce. Dip the chicken pieces into the egg mixture, then into the crumbs, completely coating the chicken. Place on a large rimmed cookie sheet or in a 9" × 13" baking dish that has been coated with nonstick vegetable spray. Bake for 25 to 30 minutes or until the chicken is completely cooked and the juices run clear.

NOTE: Serve with sweet-and-sour sauce or spicy mustard. And why not try this with some of the new flavored chow mein noodles that are on the market now, too?

Spicy Chicken Bake

3 to 4 servings

While the oven is on for this, why not throw in some potatoes to bake? It's no more work, and in 60 minutes, dinner is ready. It'll give you more time to visit with your guests.

1 chicken (2½ to 3 pounds), cut into 8 pieces
1 teaspoon salt
1 teaspoon pepper
1 cup chicken broth
2 tablespoons olive oil
1 tablespoon lemon juice
1 tablespoon teriyaki sauce
1 tablespoon Italian seasoning
1 teaspoon paprika
½ teaspoon onion powder
½ teaspoon dry mustard
¼ teaspoon ground ginger

Preheat the oven to 350°F. Place the chicken in a 9" × 13" baking dish and rub well with the salt and pepper. In a medium-sized bowl, combine the remaining ingredients; blend well and pour over the chicken, coating well. Bake for 1 hour, basting occasionally, until the chicken is cooked through and the juices run clear.

NOTE: Add a quick tossed salad and maybe Fancy Stuffed Zucchini (page 156) . . . Wow! What a meal!

Stuffed Cranberry Chicken Breasts

6 servings

After you make these for a special occasion, you'd better hope there's another special occasion soon so you can make them again. Your gang is going to insist that you make them again and again!

3 cups prepared stuffing
6 chicken breast halves, skin on and bone in (3 to 4 pounds)
1 can (16 ounces) whole-berry cranberry sauce
1 tablespoon lemon juice
2 tablespoons brown sugar

Preheat the oven to 350°F. Prepare the stuffing mix according to the package directions. Stuff ½ cup of stuffing underneath the skin of each chicken breast half. Pull the skin down over the stuffing to secure it in place (and keep it moist while baking). Place the chicken breasts in a 9" × 13" baking dish that has been coated with nonstick vegetable spray. In a small bowl, combine the cranberry sauce, lemon juice, and brown sugar; mix well. Spoon the cranberry mixture evenly over the breasts to cover. Bake for 55 minutes or until the juices run clear, basting occasionally.

NOTE: If you can't find chicken breasts split with the bone in and skin on, just ask the butcher. He'll be happy to get them for you!

Orange Blossoms

10 servings

*This has got to be one of the most impressive recipes in this book. Your dinner guests will love these...but they look so perfect that your guests won't believe you made them yourself! If that's the case, just tell them that **Mr. Food**® gave you a hand in the kitchen!*

10 large navel oranges
½ cup orange marmalade
1½ teaspoons salt
¼ teaspoon ground cinnamon
2 tablespoons brown sugar
2 tablespoons honey
3 cups cooked long-grain and wild rice
3 cups diced cooked chicken (dark meat is preferable)

Preheat the oven to 350°F. Cut the tops off the oranges one-quarter of the way down; reserve the tops for another use (see Note). Scoop out the insides of the oranges and set aside the shells. In a large bowl, combine the orange marmalade, salt, cinnamon, brown sugar, and honey. Add the rice and chicken; mix well. You may have to cut ⅛ inch from the bottom of the oranges so that they'll stand up in the pan. Then fill each orange shell with the mixture and place in two 8-inch square baking dishes that have been coated with non-stick vegetable spray. Bake for 30 to 35 minutes or until hot and the rice begins to puff.

NOTE: Save the tops that you cut off the oranges and use them for garnish.

Dining Room Chicken

3 to 4 servings

Eating in the dining room seems to make food taste special. It could be the fond memories of all the special meals shared there—or maybe it's just that we serve different foods there. Try serving this dish for dining room meals and kitchen meals . . . it's great everywhere!

2 tablespoons Dijon-style mustard
2 tablespoons brown sugar, divided
1 whole chicken (2½ to 3 pounds)
1 tablespoon cornstarch
1 can (16 ounces) whole-berry cranberry sauce
1 can (17 ounces) apricot halves in heavy syrup, drained,
chopped, and divided, with syrup reserved

Preheat the oven to 350°F. In a small bowl, combine the mustard and 1 tablespoon of brown sugar. Rub the mixture over the entire chicken, then place the chicken, breast side up, in an 8-inch square baking dish that has been coated with nonstick vegetable spray. Cover and bake for 30 minutes. Meanwhile, in a large bowl, combine the remaining 1 tablespoon of brown sugar, the cornstarch, cranberry sauce, half the apricots, and the reserved apricot syrup; mix well. Uncover the chicken and pour the syrup mixture evenly over it; return the chicken to the oven and bake, uncovered, for 30 more minutes, or until fork-tender and the juices run clear, basting occasionally. Garnish with the remaining apricot pieces.

NOTE: These leftovers make a great special fruity chicken salad. Just cut the chicken into chunks and toss with mayonnaise.

Party-Time Turkey

15 to 18 servings

Nothing says "party" like a whole turkey, but who wants to carve around all the bones when guests are waiting? Using a precooked turkey breast gives you the same turkey taste and makes you look like a carving pro—and there's no waste! (It sounds like party time to me!)

2 to 2½ cups water
One 6- to 7-pound whole boneless, cooked deli turkey breast
1 can (16 ounces) whole-berry cranberry sauce
⅓ cup orange marmalade
¼ cup firmly packed brown sugar
1 teaspoon dry mustard

Shape a piece of aluminum foil into a ½-inch-high by 6-inch-diameter ring and place in the bottom of a soup pot. Pour in the water. Place the turkey breast on top of the aluminum foil ring, keeping the turkey from touching the bottom of the pot. Bring to a boil over high heat, cover, then reduce the heat to medium-low and steam for 60 to 75 minutes or until the turkey is heated through. While the turkey is steaming, place the remaining ingredients in a small saucepan. Heat over medium-low heat for 4 to 5 minutes or until hot. Remove the turkey to a platter and pour the glaze over it.

NOTE: You may need to add additional water when steaming the turkey if the water boils away, so keep a close eye on the water level.

"What's Your Beef" Tenderloin

5 to 6 servings

When I was growing up, we ate lots of beef at home. It was usually ground beef or less-expensive steak cuts. Boy, is this a nice change! Once you try this melt-in-your-mouth beef, there won't really be any need to think twice when somebody asks, "What's your beef?"

2 to 2½ pounds beef tenderloin, trimmed
1 tablespoon vegetable oil
½ teaspoon onion powder
½ teaspoon garlic powder
¼ teaspoon pepper

Preheat the oven to 350°F. Place the tenderloin on a large rimmed cookie sheet that has been coated with nonstick vegetable spray and set aside. In a small bowl, combine the remaining ingredients and rub over the meat. Cook for 35 to 40 minutes for medium-rare, or until desired doneness. Remove the meat from the cookie sheet and slice across the grain into ½-inch slices. Serve with Shortcut Béarnaise Sauce (see next page).

NOTE: A whole tenderloin of beef will weigh between 4 and 7 pounds, but today many supermarkets are selling tenderloin in 2- to 3-pound pieces.

Shortcut Béarnaise Sauce

1 cup

Béarnaise sauce is the fancy sauce that's usually served with filet mignon. It's typically a lot of work, but this is a shortcut version that has the same big taste and will make your guests think you went to French cooking school.

2 tablespoons white vinegar
1½ teaspoons ground dried tarragon
¼ teaspoon garlic powder
½ teaspoon chopped fresh parsley
1 cup mayonnaise

In a small saucepan, combine the vinegar, tarragon, garlic powder, and parsley; simmer over medium heat for 1 to 2 minutes, stirring occasionally. Place the mayonnaise in a small bowl and add the vinegar and spice mixture; blend until smooth and creamy.

NOTE: Serve over cooked beef or veal as the perfect fresh accent.

Mustard and Black Pepper Steak

6 to 8 servings

This recipe was tested and retested because it was originally meant to be served hot, but when I tried some leftovers right from the refrigerator, I liked the taste even better! What do you think?

½ cup Italian dressing
3 tablespoons Dijon-style mustard
2 teaspoons coarsely ground black pepper
2 to 2½ pounds top round beef steak, about 1½ inches thick

In a 9" × 13" glass baking dish, combine the Italian dressing, mustard, and pepper. Place the steak in the baking dish and turn 2 or 3 times to coat completely. Cover and refrigerate for at least 2 hours, turning occasionally. Place the steak in a medium-sized metal roasting pan and broil in a preheated broiler for 8 to 10 minutes per side or until desired doneness. Cut across the grain into thin slices and serve with the sauce from the pan.

NOTE: This steak is great on sandwiches with some more Dijon mustard.

Garlic Roast

6 to 8 servings

Too often a roast has loads of flavor on the outside, and none in the center. Not this one! It's got something different—the center is stuffed with roasted garlic. Wow! (You sure won't have to worry about vampires!)

One 3- to 3½-pound beef eye of round roast
1 tablespoon plus 2 teaspoons vegetable oil, divided
8 to 10 whole garlic cloves, peeled
1 teaspoon paprika
½ teaspoon onion powder
¾ teaspoon salt
½ teaspoon pepper

Preheat the oven to 350°F. Using a long, thin knife, carefully make a horizontal slit through the center of the roast. Twist the knife gently to make a ½-inch hole. (The hole doesn't have to stay open on its own because it's going to be stuffed with garlic.) In a small saucepan, heat the 2 teaspoons of oil over medium-high heat. Sauté the garlic cloves for 3 to 4 minutes, until lightly browned, stirring often. Remove from the heat and allow to cool. In a small bowl, combine the remaining ingredients except the roast; mix well and set aside. When the garlic is cool enough to handle, push the cloves into the hole in the center of the roast until they fill the hole. Rub the oil mixture over the entire roast and place in a 7" × 11" baking dish. Roast for 60 to 75 minutes or until a meat thermometer inserted in the center indicates 160°F. for medium, or cook until desired doneness.

Orange Grove Steak

4 to 6 servings

In South Florida, where I live, one of the freshest flavors has to be oranges picked right from the tree. I wanted people to be able to enjoy that fresh goodness... even if they didn't have any orange trees outside! It's a taste that's good enough for the fanciest company.

1 cup orange marmalade
1 tablespoon orange zest
2 teaspoons soy sauce
1 teaspoon garlic powder
1 teaspoon ground dried thyme
1½ teaspoons seasoned salt
¼ teaspoon cayenne pepper
One 2- to 2½-pound top round steak, cut 1½ inches thick

In a medium-sized bowl, combine all the ingredients except the steak; mix well. Place the steak in a 9" × 13" metal baking pan. Pour the sauce over the steak and turn the steak 2 or 3 times to coat well. Place under a preheated broiler for 8 to 10 minutes per side for medium-rare or until desired doneness. Cut thin slices across the grain and serve with the sauce from the pan.

NOTE: The best way to test this for doneness is to use a meat thermometer. It should register 140°F. for rare, 160°F. for medium, and 170°F. to 180°F. for well-done.

Mustard-Glazed Tenderloin

5 to 6 servings

I've heard of mustard on hot dogs and mustard on ham, but on tenderloin? Yup, on tenderloin. No, it's not served on a bun or on rye bread, but on a platter for your dinner guests to marvel at.

2 to 2½ pounds beef tenderloin, trimmed
1 tablespoon spicy prepared mustard
2 tablespoons mayonnaise
¼ teaspoon salt
½ teaspoon garlic powder
¼ teaspoon ground dried thyme

Preheat the oven to 350°F. Place the tenderloin in a 9" × 13" baking dish. In a small bowl, combine the remaining ingredients and rub all over the meat. Bake for 35 to 40 minutes for medium-rare, or until desired doneness. Cut into ½-inch-thick slices and serve.

NOTE: You may want to mix up an extra bowl of the glaze and serve it chilled on the side as a dipping sauce.

Roast Prime Rib of Beef

8 to 10 servings

Are you one of those people who thinks it's just too hard to make prime rib at home? Think it's too restaurant-fancy? Well, if that's you, you're in for a big surprise. All it takes is a few ingredients and a few hours in the oven—and you've got what it takes to make a simple dinner into a gangbuster success.

One 4- to 6-pound boneless beef rib eye or Delmonico roast
½ teaspoon garlic powder
½ teaspoon onion powder
1 tablespoon salt
½ teaspoon pepper

Preheat the oven to 350°F. In a large roasting pan, place the beef fat side up. In a small bowl, combine the remaining ingredients; mix well. Rub the spice blend evenly over the surface of the meat. Place a meat thermometer so that the tip is centered in the roast but does not touch the fat or the bone. Roast the beef for 14 to 15 minutes per pound until the thermometer reaches 140°F. for medium-rare or until desired doneness. Remove the beef to a cutting board and let stand for 15 to 20 minutes before carving across the grain. Serve with the pan drippings.

NOTE: You can slice the roast 1 inch thick for a nice hearty dinner, or you can slice it thinner for sandwiches. And why not try it with some Shortcut Béarnaise Sauce (page 116)? Mmm!

Perfect Peachy Pork Tenderloin

4 to 6 servings

I betcha you can't say the name of this recipe three times fast—but I won't betcha you'll have any leftovers!

2 pork tenderloins (1¼ to 1½ pounds each) (not pork loin)
1 can (16 ounces) peaches in heavy syrup, coarsely chopped
½ cup ketchup
¼ cup white vinegar
½ cup firmly packed dark brown sugar
1 tablespoon chili powder
1 teaspoon garlic powder
1 tablespoon salt

Preheat the oven to 350°F. Place the pork in a 9" × 13" baking dish; set aside. In a medium-sized saucepan over medium heat, combine the remaining ingredients and bring to a boil. Pour the sauce mixture over the pork. Cover with aluminum foil and bake for 30 minutes. Reduce the heat to 325°F., uncover, and cook for 30 more minutes. Slice across the grain in ¼-inch- to ½-inch-thick slices and serve with the sauce.

NOTE: Don't skimp when serving the sauce, because it has so much flavor and looks so great!

Stuffed Pork Chop "Roast"

6 servings

Pork chops aren't typically on the menu for company because they usually dry out in the oven. Not anymore! The stuffing and sauce in this recipe keep the chops moist—so now you've got a new recipe for company.

1 box (8 ounces) one-step stuffing mix
2 teaspoons poultry seasoning
1½ teaspoons salt
1 teaspoon pepper
6 pork chops (about 2½ pounds total), each cut ¾ inch thick
1 jar (12 ounces) apricot preserves
1 can (8 ounces) jellied cranberry sauce (1 cup)
3 tablespoons vegetable oil

Preheat the oven to 350°F. Prepare the stuffing mix according to the package directions; set aside. In a small bowl or cup, combine the poultry seasoning, salt, and pepper. Rub the mixture evenly into both sides of the pork chops; set aside. In a medium-sized saucepan, heat the apricot preserves and cranberry sauce over medium-low heat until heated through and well blended. In a large skillet, heat the oil over medium heat until hot, then cook the pork chops (3 at a time) for 4 to 5 minutes, until browned on both sides. Remove the cooked chops from the pan and set aside with all the bones facing the same direction. Continue with the remaining chops. Divide the stuffing evenly over 5 of the chops. Place one chop over the next until the 5 are stacked on top of each other with the bones facing the same direction. Top with the final undressed chop. Place the entire stack on its side in an 8-inch square baking dish that has been coated with nonstick vegetable spray. If necessary, use large toothpicks or a skewer to hold the chops in place. Pour the sauce mixture over the chops and bake, covered, for 50 minutes. Remove from the oven and allow to stand for 15 minutes. Place the "roast" on a serving platter and "carve" it right at the table in front of your company.

NOTE: Serve these with extra sauce from the bottom of the baking dish.

Creamy Basil Pork Chops

4 to 6 servings

If you have pork chops in the refrigerator, you can turn them into a one-pan gourmet treat in no time with just a few other ingredients.

4 tablespoons olive oil, divided
4 garlic cloves, minced
6 pork loin chops (2½ to 3 pounds total), cut ½ inch thick
2 teaspoons dried basil
½ teaspoon salt
¼ teaspoon pepper
½ cup heavy cream

In a large skillet, heat 3 tablespoons of the olive oil over medium-high heat. Add the garlic and sauté for 1 to 2 minutes, then add the pork chops and sauté on both sides for 6 to 7 minutes per side over medium heat, until brown on both sides. Meanwhile, in a small bowl, combine the remaining 1 tablespoon olive oil, the basil, salt, and pepper. Add to the skillet 3 to 4 minutes before the chops are done, spreading the mixture around the pan and turning the chops to coat with the basil mixture. When the chops are cooked through, remove to a serving plate. Whisk the cream into the pan drippings for 2 to 3 minutes over medium heat, until the sauce thickens slightly. Pour the sauce over the cooked chops and serve immediately.

NOTE: In the summertime, pick up some fresh basil and add 2 tablespoons chopped fresh basil in place of the dried for a special treat.

Anytime Ham

10 to 12 servings

Get a jump-start on meals for the week ahead by cooking this on the weekend and enjoying the leftovers all week long.

One 4- to 5-pound smoked semi-boneless ham
1 can (29 ounces) yams, drained
2 cans (15 ounces each) whole white potatoes, drained
1 can (29 ounces) peach halves in heavy syrup,
drained and syrup reserved
1 can (16 ounces) apricot halves in heavy syrup,
drained and syrup reserved
¾ cup maple syrup
1 teaspoon dry mustard
⅛ teaspoon ground ginger
3 tablespoons cornstarch

Preheat the oven to 400°F. Trim the ham of all excess fat and place cut side down in a large roasting pan. Bake for 45 minutes, then drain off any pan drippings and reduce the heat to 350°F. Meanwhile, place the yams, white potatoes, peaches, and apricots in a large bowl and toss gently; set aside. In a medium-sized saucepan, over medium-high heat, combine 1 cup of the reserved peach syrup, ½ cup of the reserved apricot syrup, the maple syrup, dry mustard, and ginger; bring to a boil, then remove from the heat. In a small bowl, mix 3 more tablespoons of the reserved apricot or peach syrup with the cornstarch and add to the hot syrup mixture, stirring until it thickens. Place the potatoes and fruit around the ham and pour the syrup mixture over everything in the pan. Bake for 35 to 45 more minutes, uncovered, basting occasionally.

NOTE: Carve the ham across the grain. Any leftover ham is ideal for sandwiches.

Salmon Lovers' Salmon

5 to 6 servings

Attention, salmon lovers! Here's one I bet you didn't think you could make at home without fancy kitchen equipment. And with only three ingredients, you'll be wanting to poach up a storm.

One 2-pound fresh salmon fillet
1 lemon, sliced ½ inch thick
½ cup dry white wine

Preheat the oven to 350°F. Place a 16- to 18-inch-long piece of aluminum foil in a large roasting pan; place the salmon on the foil and bring up the sides of the foil. Place the lemon slices on top of the salmon and pour the wine over the top. Wrap the foil tightly around the fish and fill the roasting pan with ½ inch of warm water. Bake for 30 to 35 minutes, until the fish is cooked through. Carefully unwrap the fish and remove the lemon slices. Serve warm or cold with fresh-squeezed lemon, Patient Dill Sauce (see next page), a prepared mayonnaise-mustard blend, or maybe a combination of bottled ranch salad dressing and sour cream.

NOTE: A 2-pound salmon fillet is 1 large piece of boneless salmon. Ask for it at your local fish market or at your supermarket fish department.

 Mr. Food®'s "take-along" suggestion

Patient Dill Sauce

1 cup

This is a keep-on-hand sauce that can be made up and kept in the refrigerator, waiting till you're ready to use it. It goes with almost anything, so I doubt you can be patient, knowing its fresh taste is waiting right at your fingertips.

½ cup mayonnaise
½ cup sour cream
1 tablespoon chopped fresh dillweed
⅛ teaspoon dry mustard

In a small bowl, combine all of the ingredients; mix well. Serve immediately or cover and chill until ready to use.

NOTE: No fresh dillweed? Use 1 teaspoon dried dill in its place. This sauce should last in your fridge for up to 3 weeks if kept in an airtight container.

Angelic Seafood

4 servings

Do you think there's a relationship between the name of this recipe and the fact that it tastes so heavenly?

8 ounces uncooked angel hair pasta
½ cup (1 stick) butter
1 medium-sized red bell pepper, seeded and cut into ¼-inch strips
1 medium-sized green bell pepper, seeded and
cut into ¼-inch strips
1 medium-sized onion, chopped (about 1 cup)
1 can (2 ounces) anchovy fillets, chopped
3 teaspoons minced garlic (6 to 8 cloves)
1 teaspoon salt
½ teaspoon black pepper
8 ounces bay scallops
12 ounces medium-sized cooked, peeled, and deveined shrimp

In a large pot of boiling salted water, cook the pasta according to the package directions; drain and keep warm in a large serving bowl. Meanwhile, in a large skillet, melt the butter over medium-high heat; add the bell peppers and onion and sauté for 5 to 6 minutes or until the edges of the peppers begin to brown. Stir in the anchovies, garlic, salt, and black pepper and sauté for 3 to 4 more minutes. Add the scallops and shrimp and sauté for 3 to 5 minutes, until the scallops are cooked and the shrimp is heated through. Pour over the drained pasta and toss.

NOTE: I like a big anchovy taste. If you do, too, add an additional can of anchovies to the recipe.

Entertaining Side Dishes

We all have our favorite side dishes . . . and we know side dishes can give that extra touch that'll turn a good meal into a great one. But every so often we get into a rut with the same side dishes and want some new taste combinations.

Help has arrived! There are so many sassy side dishes here for you to choose from! There are pages of pasta, rice, potatoes, and vegetables. Some are new ideas, like Potato and Cheese Snowballs (page 147) and Roasted Plum Tomatoes (page 151), and others are great twists on old favorites, like Spiral Baked Potatoes (page 144) and Vegetable Dill Stir-Fry (page 154).

Your guests and family will be thrilled with these! They're all exciting, fresh, and, as always, a snap to prepare. Remember, you can serve two or three side dishes for your dinner so that the whole gang can choose their favorites. I wonder which ones you'll choose tonight . . .

ENTERTAINING SIDE DISHES

Mr. Food®'s "take-along" suggestion

Baked Potato Buffet

Surprise your company with a meal that's fun to "build" *and* fun to eat—stuffed baked potatoes. All you have to do is bake 1 large baking potato per person, set them out with a selection of your favorite toppings (see page 137 for suggestions), and let your guests construct their own potato creations.

Terrific Tips for Making Perfect Baked Potatoes

- Always scrub potato skins well under cold, running water.
- Prick potatoes with a fork before baking to shorten the baking time.
- Here's another way to cut down on baking time: Insert a heated metal skewer through each potato and leave it in during baking. (Heating the skewer first "seals" the potato and prevents it from turning dark in the center.) Be careful when inserting and removing the hot skewers.
- Rub a bit of olive or vegetable oil on the outside of the potatoes before baking to make their skins crispy.
- Do *not* wrap potatoes in aluminum foil for baking. Foil holds in moisture and steams potatoes, resulting in a "boiled" taste and texture.
- Turn the potatoes over halfway through the baking time to prevent browning of the undersides where they touch the baking tray or oven rack.

- Bake potatoes in a 400°F. oven for 55 to 60 minutes or until soft.
- To "bake" potatoes in the microwave, wash but don't dry them. Pierce, then wrap them in microwave-safe paper towels and place 1 inch apart on a microwave rack. Cook according to your oven's guidelines, turning potatoes once during cooking. Don't exceed the cooking time because potatoes will continue to cook after they're removed from the oven. **Be sure *not* to use metal skewers or aluminum foil in the microwave.**
- If baking more than 10 potatoes at a time, it's best to use the conventional oven method instead of the microwave.
- A baked potato is ready when a fork easily pierces its skin. If the potato is hard, bake it a little longer. However, be careful not to overbake, or the underskin will dry up.
- If potatoes baked to doneness are being held for over 10 minutes before serving, wrap them in foil. This will enhance the appearance of the skin by reducing shriveling.
- Instead of using a knife to open a baked potato (a knife flattens the surface and alters the normally fluffy texture of a baked spud), insert the tines of a fork in a straight line through the top of the potato, then press the ends toward the center to "pop" it open. Be careful—you may need to hold on to the potato with a napkin if it's too hot to handle.

Potato Toppers

There are lots of fun toppings you can use on your baked potato buffet. You can top baked potatoes with almost anything. Did you ever think of topping them with leftover stews and cream-style soups? Why not try them with Cauliflower and Broccoli Melt (page 148), Creamed Spinach (page 153), and Lovin' Onions (page 150). . . . Yummy! My favorite simple toppings are:

- sour cream
- shredded cheese
- gravy
- chili
- lightly cooked vegetables (even frozen and canned veggies are topping winners)

If you want to keep them healthy, it's easy, since potatoes are naturally low in fat and calories. You can keep them that way by offering lowfat toppings to go along with them, such as:

- plain nonfat yogurt with chopped scallions
- lowfat cottage cheese and chives
- stewed tomatoes
- steamed broccoli florets or julienned carrots
- spicy mustard or salsa

As I always say, you know your own dos and don'ts, likes and dislikes, so do your own thing!

Tarragon Red Potatoes

8 to 10 servings

You thought all those expensive restaurants had some secret recipe for their red potatoes... but all you need to enjoy them the same way at home are some candles and a tablecloth. Watch out! You're in for a four-star meal.

1½ teaspoons ground dried tarragon
¼ cup olive oil
½ teaspoon garlic powder
1½ teaspoons salt
¼ teaspoon pepper
3 pounds red potatoes, cut into 1-inch pieces

In a small bowl, combine all of the ingredients except the potatoes; mix well. Place the potatoes in a large bowl; pour the mixture over them and toss to coat evenly. Place the potatoes on a rimmed cookie sheet and bake for 75 to 90 minutes, or until the potatoes are tender inside and crispy outside, turning the potatoes halfway through the cooking.

NOTE: I like to leave the skin on my red potatoes—they just need to be cleaned well first.

Smashed Potatoes

6 to 8 servings

"Smashing"! Absolutely "smashing"!

4 pounds red potatoes, unpeeled
½ cup (1 stick) butter
1 cup (½ pint) sour cream
¼ cup milk
½ teaspoon onion powder
1¾ teaspoons salt
¼ teaspoon white pepper

Place the potatoes in a soup pot and add enough water to cover the potatoes by about ¾ inch. Bring to a boil over high heat, then reduce the heat to medium and cook for 20 to 25 minutes or until the potatoes are fork-tender; drain and place the potatoes in a large bowl. Add the remaining ingredients and "smash" the potatoes with a potato masher, or if you like them smoother, with an electric mixer.

NOTE: These can be placed in a 2-quart casserole dish and kept warm in the oven at 250°F. for an hour, or until ready to serve.

Potato Corn Bake

8 to 10 servings

Veggies and potatoes in one dish—now that's entertaining made easy!

2 pounds frozen hash brown potato cubes, thawed
2 cans (15 ounces each) creamed corn
1 cup half-and-half
1 jar (2 ounces) diced pimientos
½ teaspoon seasoned salt
½ teaspoon onion powder
½ teaspoon salt
¼ teaspoon pepper
¼ cup Italian-style seasoned bread crumbs

Preheat the oven to 375°F. In a large bowl, combine all of the ingredients except the bread crumbs; mix well. Pour the mixture into a 9" × 13" baking dish that has been coated with nonstick vegetable spray. Sprinkle the bread crumbs evenly over the top. Bake for 35 to 40 minutes, until golden and heated through.

NOTE: Serve this with Good Ol' Honey-Baked Chicken (page 66) and wash it down with a glass of Frozen Lemonade Cooler (page 232).

Anytime Potatoes

10 to 12 servings

Brunch perfect, dinner perfect—a go-along for any party, any time of the day.

½ cup (1 stick) butter, melted
1 can (10¾ ounces) cream of chicken or mushroom soup
1 pint (16 ounces) sour cream
½ teaspoon dried basil
½ teaspoon onion powder
¼ teaspoon pepper
¼ teaspoon ground cumin
½ teaspoon garlic powder
2 pounds frozen hash brown potato cubes, thawed
¼ cup dry bread crumbs
½ cup grated Parmesan cheese

Preheat the oven to 350°F. Place the melted butter in a large bowl and add the remaining ingredients except the potatoes, bread crumbs, and Parmesan; mix well. Add the potatoes and stir until evenly coated. Press the potato mixture into a 9" × 13" baking dish that has been coated with nonstick vegetable spray. Sprinkle with the bread crumbs and the cheese. Bake for 75 to 85 minutes or until hot and bubbly.

NOTE: Serve these with Egg and Cheese Biscuit Bake (page 40) for a super brunch combo.

Double Stuffers

6 servings

These might be a little extra work, but they're definitely worth the effort. I'm sure your guests will agree!

6 large baking potatoes
½ teaspoon salt
¼ teaspoon pepper
¼ cup sour cream
3 tablespoons butter
¼ teaspoon onion powder
Paprika for sprinkling

Preheat the oven to 400°F. Scrub the potatoes and pierce the skins with a fork. Bake for 55 minutes or until tender. Slice about ½ inch off the top of each potato and scoop out the pulp; place the pulp in a medium-sized bowl. Add the salt, pepper, sour cream, butter, and onion powder and beat with an electric mixer. Spoon back into the potato shells and lightly sprinkle the tops with paprika. Bake for 30 minutes or until the potatoes start to brown on top.

NOTE: These can be prepared and frozen for up to 1 month before baking, if wrapped well. Just thaw in the refrigerator overnight and bake as directed.

Parmesan Potato Sticks

5 to 6 servings

Having a buffet or potluck dinner and need a potato dish that'll go with everything? This is it! It'll surely get a big thumbs up!

½ cup dry bread crumbs
½ cup grated Parmesan cheese
⅛ teaspoon garlic powder
½ teaspoon salt
⅛ teaspoon pepper
2 pounds baking potatoes
½ cup (1 stick) butter, melted

Preheat the oven to 400°F. In a small bowl, mix together the bread crumbs, Parmesan, garlic powder, salt, and pepper; set aside. Peel the potatoes and cut lengthwise into quarters; cut each quarter lengthwise into 3 strips. Dip each strip in the melted butter, then in the Parmesan mixture, making sure the potatoes are well coated. Place in a single layer in a large baking dish (or dishes) that has been coated with nonstick vegetable spray. Pour any remaining melted butter over the potatoes. Bake for 30 to 35 minutes, until the potatoes are tender, turning them once or twice.

NOTE: It's not often that it's okay to eat potatoes with your fingers (unless they're French fries). These are tasty exceptions!

Spiral Baked Potatoes

6 servings

Here's a new way to show off your kitchen know-how. You'll have everybody wondering just how you made these!

6 large baking potatoes
3 tablespoons vegetable oil
½ teaspoon salt
½ teaspoon pepper
3 slices (1 ounce each) Cheddar cheese, cut in half
2 tablespoons chopped scallions or chives

Preheat the oven to 400°F. Put 2 wooden spoons parallel to one another on a work surface and place a potato lengthwise between the handles. Make 8 crosswise slits three fourths of the way through the potato, stopping each time the knife hits the spoon handles. Repeat with the remaining potatoes; set aside. In a small bowl, combine the oil, salt, and pepper; rub the mixture evenly over the potatoes. Place the potatoes cut sides up on a cookie sheet and bake for 55 to 60 minutes or until tender. Remove from the oven and place a cut piece of Cheddar cheese on top of each potato; bake for 2 to 3 more minutes, until the cheese is melted. Sprinkle with the chopped scallions and serve.

NOTE: If you'd like, add some sour cream and/or bacon bits to make these even more special.

Potato Salad Confetti Mold

8 to 10 servings

Did you think that confetti was only for New Year's and birthdays? Not anymore! With this recipe, there's a new reason to celebrate!

6 medium-sized white potatoes, peeled and cut into 1-inch cubes
(about 2½ pounds)
2 hard-boiled eggs, chopped
1 cup chopped celery (2 stalks)
1 can (2.25 ounces) sliced black olives, drained (½ cup)
1 small red bell pepper, chopped (about ½ cup)
1 small red onion, chopped (about ½ cup)
1 cup mayonnaise
½ teaspoon salt
½ teaspoon black pepper
1 envelope (0.25 ounces) unflavored gelatin
¼ cup boiling water

Place the potato cubes in a large saucepan and fill with enough water to cover the potatoes. Bring to a boil over medium-high heat and cook for 15 to 20 minutes, until fork-tender; drain and cool. In a large bowl, combine the eggs, celery, black olives, bell pepper, onion, mayonnaise, salt, and black pepper; set aside. Dissolve the gelatin in the boiling water; cool. Add the cooled gelatin to the celery mixture; mix well. Add the potatoes and stir until evenly coated. Pour into a 9-inch loaf pan and refrigerate for at least 3 to 4 hours. Invert the pan onto a large oval platter, gently shaking the mold to loosen it. Slice into serving-sized pieces.

     Mr. Food®'s "take-along" suggestion

Potato and Cheese Snowballs

12 servings

These won't melt in the heat, but they will disappear once your gang gets ahold of them.

6 tablespoons (¾ stick) butter, divided
1 pound frozen shredded hash brown potatoes, thawed
1 medium-sized onion, chopped (about 1 cup)
1 tablespoon minced garlic
½ cup (2 ounces) shredded mozzarella cheese
½ cup (2 ounces) shredded Monterey Jack cheese
¼ teaspoon Italian seasoning
1 teaspoon salt
¼ teaspoon pepper

In a large nonstick skillet, heat half of the butter over medium heat. Add the potatoes and cook, turning frequently, for 12 to 15 minutes, until browned. Place in a large bowl and set aside. In the same skillet, heat the remaining butter, then add the onions and garlic and sauté until golden, being careful not to burn. Add the browned onions and garlic to the potatoes. Add the remaining ingredients; mix well. Preheat the broiler. Using an ice cream scoop, scoop out the potatoes into 12 equal-sized scoops, packing tightly, and place the scoops on a cookie sheet that has been coated with nonstick vegetable spray. Broil until browned and hot.

NOTE: After these are finished, they can be cooled, covered, and refrigerated overnight for brunch the next day or for a great dinner side dish. Just reheat in a 300°F. oven for 10 to 15 minutes or until heated through.

Cauliflower and Broccoli Melt

6 servings

This reminds me of a bubbly casserole that my grandmother always made. It'll have your family smiling and begging for more, just like my family always did!

1 bag (16 ounces) frozen broccoli florets, thawed and drained
1 bag (16 ounces) frozen cauliflower, thawed and drained
1 cup mayonnaise
3 tablespoons Dijon-style mustard
½ teaspoon salt
½ cup (2 ounces) shredded Cheddar cheese

Preheat the oven to 375°F. In a large bowl, combine all the ingredients except the cheese and mix until the vegetables are evenly coated. Place in a 1½-quart casserole dish that has been coated with nonstick vegetable spray and sprinkle with the cheese. Bake for 25 to 30 minutes or until heated through and the cheese is melted.

NOTE: This makes a great topping for baked potatoes (see page 137).

     Mr. Food®'s "take-along" suggestion

Corn Pudding

When you entertain you always want to try to serve something different. This one should be a welcome change!

1 cup milk
4 eggs, well beaten
2 tablespoons butter
¾ teaspoon salt
¼ teaspoon white pepper
½ cup biscuit baking mix
2 cans (15 to 17 ounces each) whole kernel corn, drained
2 tablespoons chopped bottled or canned jalapeño peppers,
drained

Preheat the oven to 375°F. In a medium-sized saucepan, over low heat, combine the milk, eggs, butter, salt, and pepper; stir until the butter has melted. Do not overheat or the mixture will congeal. Remove from the heat, stir in the biscuit baking mix, corn, and jalapeño peppers. Pour into an 8-inch square baking dish that has been coated with nonstick vegetable spray. Bake for 50 minutes or until golden brown and the center is set.

NOTE: Cut or scoop into serving-sized portions.

Lovin' Onions

8 to 10 servings

*If you've never eaten onions baked like this…boy, are you in for a treat!
You're gonna love 'em (and you'll love how easy they are)!*

1 tablespoon butter
7 medium-sized sweet onions, coarsely chopped (about 7 cups)
½ cup self-rising flour
½ teaspoon salt
¼ teaspoon pepper
1¼ cups (5 ounces) shredded Cheddar cheese, divided
1¼ cups (5 ounces) shredded Monterey Jack cheese, divided
1 tablespoon chopped bottled or canned jalapeño peppers, drained

Preheat the oven to 350°F. In a large skillet, melt the butter over medium-high heat. Add the onions and sauté for about 10 minutes, until softened. Meanwhile, in a medium-sized bowl, combine the flour, salt, and pepper. Add 1 cup of each cheese; mix well. Add the jalapeño peppers and the cooked onions; mix well. Pour into a 1½-quart casserole dish that has been coated with nonstick vegetable spray. Combine the remaining cheeses and sprinkle evenly over the onion mixture. Bake for 30 minutes or until the cheese is melted and bubbly.

NOTE: If you're serving these right from the casserole dish on the kitchen or dining room table, be sure to use a trivet.

Roasted Plum Tomatoes

5 to 6 servings

You want a versatile recipe? Stop here. These roasted tomatoes can be served by themselves as a side dish, or as a topping for cooked pasta, rice, or potatoes—or almost anything! See, I told you they're versatile!

1 tablespoon vegetable oil
1 teaspoon salt
¼ teaspoon pepper
¼ teaspoon garlic powder
¼ teaspoon onion powder
10 to 12 plum tomatoes

Preheat the oven to 450°F. In a medium-sized bowl, combine all the ingredients except the tomatoes. Cut the tomatoes lengthwise and squeeze out the seeds and juice. Toss in the oil mixture and place in a 7" × 11" baking dish. Bake for 20 to 25 minutes or until tender but not overcooked.

NOTE: For a whole new taste, sprinkle these with ½ cup of your favorite shredded cheese right after they come out of the oven, then return them to the oven for 3 to 4 more minutes, until the cheese is melted.

Creamed Spinach

6 to 8 servings

Spinach has been making a real comeback. When it's made like this, you'll know why!

4 ounces (4 slices) uncooked bacon, chopped
1 medium-sized onion, finely chopped (about 1 cup)
¼ cup all-purpose flour
2 teaspoons seasoned salt
¼ teaspoon onion powder
½ teaspoon salt
¼ teaspoon pepper
⅛ teaspoon ground nutmeg
2 cups milk
2 packages (10 ounces each) frozen spinach,
thawed and squeezed dry

In a large skillet, cook the bacon over medium-high heat until almost crisp. Add the onion and cook for 5 to 7 minutes, until the onion is softened. Remove from the heat and add the flour, seasoned salt, onion powder, salt, pepper, and nutmeg; blend well. Gradually stir in the milk and cook over low heat until thickened. Add the spinach and cook until heated through, stirring constantly.

NOTE: For the best results, make sure the spinach is well drained. This also makes a gangbuster topping for baked potatoes (see page 137).

Three-Corn Bake

8 servings

Is it stuffing? Is it corn bread? All I know is, it's a favorite at my house!

1 can (15 to 17 ounces) whole kernel corn, undrained
1 can (15 ounces) creamed corn
1 box (8½ ounces) corn muffin mix
1 cup (½ pint) sour cream
1 egg, beaten

Preheat the oven to 350°F. In a medium-sized bowl, combine all the ingredients; mix well. Pour into a 1½-quart casserole dish that has been coated with nonstick vegetable spray. Bake for 60 to 65 minutes or until the center is set. Allow to cool for 15 minutes before serving.

NOTE: This is best served with poultry. What a hearty combo!

Vegetable Dill Stir-Fry

6 to 8 servings

I've shared quite a few Asian-style stir-fry dishes with you, but now it's time for a crispy, fresh garden version.

2 tablespoons peanut oil
2 green bell peppers, seeded and cut into ¼-inch strips
2 red bell peppers, seeded and cut into ¼-inch strips
2 medium-sized onions, cut into ¼-inch half-moons
6 stalks celery, cut into ½-inch diagonal slices
1 can (15 ounces) baby corn, drained
1 can (5 ounces) sliced water chestnuts, drained
½ cup chicken stock
Juice of 1 lemon (2 to 3 tablespoons)
1 tablespoon cornstarch
½ teaspoon dried dill
½ teaspoon salt

In an extra-large skillet or a wok, heat the oil over medium-high heat. Add the peppers, onions, celery, and corn and toss to coat with the oil. Cook for 10 to 12 minutes, stirring occasionally, until the vegetables are cooked but still firm. In a small bowl, combine the remaining ingredients; pour into the vegetable mixture and cook for 5 to 6 more minutes or until desired doneness.

NOTE: A perfect side dish for Chinese Almond Noodle Chicken (page 109).

Cauliflower Blossom

6 to 8 servings

Serving the cauliflower whole and carving it at the table looks really impressive . . . just like when you carve the turkey!

1 medium-sized head of cauliflower, trimmed
¼ cup seasoned bread crumbs
¼ cup grated Parmesan cheese
1 teaspoon dried dill
¼ teaspoon salt
⅛ teaspoon pepper
Nonstick vegetable spray
¼ cup (½ stick) butter, melted

Preheat the oven to 350°F. In a soup pot, heat ½ inch water to boiling. Place the whole trimmed cauliflower stem side down in the pot. Cover and steam over medium heat for 12 to 15 minutes or until tender. Meanwhile, in a small bowl, combine the bread crumbs, Parmesan, dill, salt, and pepper; set aside. After the cauliflower has steamed, carefully remove it to an 8-inch square baking dish that has been coated with nonstick vegetable spray. Pour the melted butter evenly over the top. Cover the top of the cauliflower with the bread crumb mixture, pressing it onto the cauliflower so that it sticks. Spray the entire cauliflower with additional nonstick vegetable spray. Bake for 40 to 45 minutes, until the crumbs are lightly browned and the cauliflower is fork-tender.

NOTE: You'll want to serve this with extra melted butter for dipping.

Fancy Stuffed Zucchini

6 to 8 servings

This dish is so elegant and delicious that your guests will be peeking into the kitchen to see if you had dinner catered!

4 medium to large zucchini
¼ cup vegetable oil
2 garlic cloves, minced
4 small carrots, grated (about 1 cup)
1 small onion, chopped (about ½ cup)
½ teaspoon salt
¼ teaspoon pepper
1½ cups seasoned bread crumbs
⅓ cup grated Parmesan cheese

Preheat the oven to 375°F. Wash the zucchini and remove the ends. Slice each zucchini lengthwise and scoop out the centers, reserving the pulp. In a medium-sized skillet, heat the oil over medium-high heat. Add the garlic and sauté for 1 minute. Add the reserved zucchini pulp, the carrots, onion, salt, and pepper. Cook for 8 to 10 minutes, until the zucchini is softened. Place in a large bowl and add the bread crumbs and Parmesan; mix well. Stuff the zucchini shells with the bread mixture. Place in a 9" × 13" baking dish that has been coated with nonstick vegetable spray. Bake for 30 to 35 minutes or until the zucchini shells are fork-tender and the tops begin to brown.

NOTE: Serve whole at a buffet or cut into serving-sized portions for family-style meals.

Garden Loaf

4 to 6 servings

Here's a way to turn your favorite veggies into an all-vegetable version of meat loaf. And it's so simple you might wanna make 2 or 3 so you can have them on hand in the freezer.

1 medium-sized onion, finely chopped (about 1 cup)
2 stalks celery, finely chopped (about 1 cup)
2 medium-sized carrots, grated (about 1 cup)
½ of a medium-sized green bell pepper, finely chopped
(about ¼ cup)
1 cup finely chopped walnuts
1 cup dry bread crumbs
½ teaspoon salt
½ teaspoon black pepper
½ teaspoon dried dill
½ cup mayonnaise
2 eggs, slightly beaten

Preheat the oven to 350°F. Line an 8" × 4" loaf pan with aluminum foil. Coat the foil with nonstick vegetable spray. In a large bowl, combine the onion, celery, carrots, green pepper, walnuts, bread crumbs, salt, black pepper, and dill. In a small bowl, mix the mayonnaise and eggs until smooth; stir into the vegetable mixture until well mixed, then pour into the prepared pan and bake for 45 to 50 minutes or until lightly browned. Let cool in the pan for about 15 minutes, then invert the loaf and remove the foil. Place right-side up on a serving platter and serve immediately, or cover and chill until ready to use; reheat before serving.

NOTE: This is a perfect "all-in-one" side dish that can even be served as a hearty main dish if you'd like.

Black Bean Salad

6 to 8 servings

If you want to try something new and yummy, this one is for you. Black beans are really "in" right now, so come on and be a trendsetter.

1 medium-sized head of iceberg lettuce, shredded (about 8 cups)
1 can (15 ounces) black beans, rinsed and drained
1 medium-sized red bell pepper, chopped (about ¾ cup)
1 small onion, chopped (about ½ cup)
⅓ cup olive oil
2 tablespoons lemon juice
1 teaspoon garlic powder
2 tablespoons chopped fresh parsley
¼ teaspoon salt
¼ teaspoon black pepper

In a large bowl, combine all of the ingredients; mix well. Serve immediately or cover and chill until ready to use.

NOTE: What a super side dish for a summertime picnic or backyard barbecue!

Marinated Mushrooms

5 to 6 servings

These are so easy, you won't believe it. And neither will your friends! They'll think you bought these at one of those fancy gourmet shops.

1 bottle (8 ounces) Italian salad dressing (1 cup)
1 tablespoon sugar
1 medium-sized onion, cut into wedges
1 tablespoon cider vinegar
1 teaspoon dried parsley flakes
1 package (10 ounces) fresh whole mushrooms, cleaned and ends trimmed

Place all of the ingredients except the mushrooms in a medium-sized glass bowl; mix well. Add the mushrooms and toss to coat. Cover and marinate in the refrigerator for at least 4 hours.

NOTE: These are a super cold side dish and, served with toothpicks, they make a refreshing hors d'oeuvre, too.

Easy Bundt Noodle Pudding

12 servings

This is so special looking on the table that you certainly won't need a centerpiece!

1 package (16 ounces) uncooked medium-sized egg noodles
6 eggs, well beaten
1 envelope (from a 2-ounce box) onion soup mix
1 cup (½ pint) sour cream
1 teaspoon salt
1 teaspoon pepper
1 package (10 ounces) frozen peas, thawed
¼ cup (½ stick) butter, melted

Preheat the oven to 350°F. In a large pot of boiling salted water, cook the noodles according to the package directions; drain, rinse with cold water, drain again, and set aside. Meanwhile, place the eggs, onion soup mix, sour cream, salt, pepper, and peas in a large bowl; mix well. Add the noodles and stir to coat. Pour the mixture into a 10-inch Bundt pan that has been coated with nonstick vegetable spray. Drizzle the melted butter evenly over the noodle mixture and bake for 60 to 70 minutes or until bubbling and the top begins to brown. Place a large plate over the Bundt pan and invert carefully. Slice into serving-sized pieces.

NOTE: Any leftovers can be tightly wrapped in plastic wrap and used the next day—still to rave reviews.

Macaroni Mold

12 to 14 servings

Pasta is an all-time favorite, and it's no wonder! You can do so many things with it. Here's just one example where it really shines.

1 package (16 ounces) uncooked elbow macaroni
2 cups mayonnaise
¾ cup sweet relish
2 small carrots, grated (about ½ cup)
½ of a small sweet onion, chopped (about ¼ cup)
1 teaspoon salt
½ teaspoon pepper
1 envelope (0.25 ounces) unflavored gelatin
¼ cup boiling water

In a large pot of boiling salted water, cook the macaroni according to the package directions; drain and cool. In a large bowl, combine the mayonnaise, relish, carrot, onion, salt, and pepper; set aside. Dissolve the gelatin in the boiling water and allow to cool for about 5 minutes. Add the gelatin and macaroni to the mayonnaise mixture; mix until evenly coated. Pour into a 10-inch Bundt pan or mold and refrigerate for 3 hours or until set. Invert the mold onto a platter and serve.

NOTE: Make this a day or two in advance when you know you'll be busy with other last-minute party preparations.

Spaghetti Rice

5 to 6 servings

"Hmm, should I serve rice? Or would pasta be better?" The answer is simple... serve both! This recipe is so little work that it'll give you a minute to relax before the gang arrives.

4 tablespoons vegetable oil, divided
1 can (4 ounces) mushroom slices or mushroom
stems and pieces, drained
1 medium-sized onion, chopped (about 1 cup)
1 cup (about 4 ounces) uncooked spaghetti,
broken into 3-inch pieces
1½ cups uncooked long- or whole-grain rice
2 cans (13¾ ounces each) chicken broth
¼ teaspoon salt
⅛ teaspoon pepper

Heat 3 tablespoons oil in a large saucepan over medium-high heat; add the mushrooms and onion and sauté until lightly browned. Remove from the pan and set aside. Heat the remaining oil in the saucepan and brown the spaghetti over medium-low heat. (Be careful—it browns quickly.) Remove the pan from the heat and put the mushrooms and onion back into the pan. Add the remaining ingredients, mixing well. Bring the mixture to a boil, reduce the heat to low, cover, and cook for 20 more minutes or until all the liquid is absorbed.

NOTE: If you're looking for a good make-ahead dish, this one freezes well.

   Mr. Food®'s "take-along" suggestion

Quick Italian Rice

6 servings

The "quick" means it'll be on the table in minutes. The "Italian" means lots of good old-fashioned flavor.

1 cup uncooked long- or whole-grain rice
2 cups chicken broth, divided
1 tablespoon butter
½ cup thinly sliced carrots
½ cup thinly sliced zucchini
½ cup thinly sliced yellow squash
¼ cup dry white wine
¼ cup grated Parmesan cheese
¼ teaspoon white pepper

In a large saucepan, combine the rice and 1½ cups of the chicken broth; bring to a boil, stirring occasionally. Reduce the heat to low, cover, and simmer for about 15 minutes; set aside. In a large skillet, melt the butter over medium-high heat and cook the carrots, zucchini, and yellow squash for 2 to 3 minutes, just until softened. Add the wine and cook for 2 more minutes; set aside and keep warm. Add the remaining ½ cup broth to the hot rice and stir over medium-high heat until the broth is absorbed. Stir in the cooked vegetables, the cheese, and pepper. Serve immediately.

Salads and More from Garden to Grove

Fruits and salads are the easiest, freshest-tasting companions for our get-togethers. And they go a long way, too, which makes them very affordable for a crowd.

Now the ones here aren't your ordinary lettuce and tomato salads. These have pizzazz—like Shrimp Scampi Salad (page 175) and B.L.T. Salad (page 174). Both are perfect as side dishes or even as fresh meals all by themselves. And how about a refreshing gelatin salad? I know, I know, they've been around for years. But I've got some that have new twists, so I think we can start our own fad with them—and are they ever easy!

Fresh fruit sure colors and brightens up a table, so why not try some Summer Citrus Mold (page 171)? Another way to enjoy our fresh fruit is in a chilled fruit soup like Fruit Soup Plus (page 169). And let's not forget that fruit can be served as a light side dish or dessert. It's tasty enough to satisfy any sweet tooth.

So, the next time you extend an invitation, why not plan to serve one of these salad, fruit, or gelatin dishes? You'll be happy because they're easy to make ahead of time, and your company will be happy 'cause they taste so incredibly good!

SALADS AND MORE FROM GARDEN TO GROVE

Mr. Food®'s "take-along" suggestion

Country Fruit Stand Salad

10 to 15 servings

My grandchildren love this, and I love making it for them! Share the country goodness with your gang.

1 medium to large cantaloupe
1 medium to large honeydew melon
1 medium to large pineapple
1 quart strawberries, washed and hulled (tops removed)
¾ cup ginger ale
½ cup orange juice
2 tablespoons honey

Slice the cantaloupe and honeydew in half. Remove the seeds and rind. Cut into 1-inch bite-sized pieces. Cut off the top of the pineapple, then slice it into quarters. Remove the core and rind from each quarter and cut into 1-inch bite-sized pieces. Place the cut fruit into a large bowl. Cut the strawberries into halves (or quarters, if they're large); add to the other fruit. In a small bowl, combine the ginger ale, orange juice, and honey; mix well. Add to the fruit and mix well; allow to "marry" for 15 to 20 minutes before serving. If not serving immediately, cover and chill until ready to use.

NOTE: There's a wide range in the amount this makes because it depends on the size of the fruit you use.

   Mr. Food®'s "take-along" suggestion

Chocolate-Laced Fruit Kebabs

10 kebabs

Mention chocolate-covered fruit, and they'll be waiting in line! Mention Chocolate-Laced Fruit Kebabs, and you'd better figure out how to handle the crowds . . . and the compliments!

10 wooden or metal skewers (each 10 to 12 inches long)

½ of a large cantaloupe
½ of a large honeydew melon
½ of a large pineapple
20 medium-sized strawberries, washed and hulled (tops removed)
½ cup semisweet chocolate chips
1 tablespoon butter
2 tablespoons light corn syrup

Cut the cantaloupe half into 5 wedges. Remove the rind and cut each wedge into 4 chunks. Repeat with the honeydew. Cut the pineapple half into 4 wedges. Remove the core and rind, then cut each wedge into 5 chunks. On each of the skewers, alternate a strawberry, honeydew chunk, cantaloupe chunk, and pineapple chunk. Repeat until 8 pieces of fruit are on each skewer. Repeat the entire process until all 10 skewers are complete. Place them on a wax paper–lined cookie sheet. In a small saucepan, combine the chocolate chips, butter, and corn syrup over low heat. Stir until the chips are melted. Drizzle about ¾ tablespoon of the chocolate mixture onto each skewer. Allow 5 minutes for the chocolate to firm up before serving, or cover and refrigerate until ready to serve.

NOTE: Not in the mood for chocolate? Make the skewers by themselves as a healthy snack or a great edible garnish.

Fruit Soup Plus

4 to 6 servings

What's the "plus"? The "plus" is the fact that you're serving something so easy that's so good for them and still so scrumptious.

1 can (8 ounces) crushed pineapple
½ cup (3 to 4 large) diced strawberries
½ pint fresh blueberries
1 cup seedless grape halves
1 cup apple juice
1 cup orange juice
1 cup pineapple juice
½ cup nonfat vanilla yogurt (optional)

In a large bowl, combine the pineapple, strawberries, blueberries, and grapes. Pour the juices over the fruit and stir well. Pour the soup into serving bowls or glasses and garnish each with a dollop of yogurt just before serving.

NOTE: If you'd like this even sweeter, add some canned fruit cocktail, honey, or extra-fine granulated sugar.

Five-a-Day Gelatin

6 servings

It's really important these days to eat 5 portions of fruits and veggies a day. This wouldn't count as a whole day's worth, but if you serve it topped with fresh fruit, you'll be on your way...

Two packages (4 servings each) strawberry-flavored gelatin
1 jar (15 ounces) applesauce
1 small can (6 ounces) frozen orange juice concentrate
1 can (12 ounces) lemon-lime soda (1½ cups)
2 medium-sized bananas, peeled and sliced ¼ inch thick

In a medium-sized saucepan, dissolve the gelatin in the applesauce over low heat, about 2 to 3 minutes. Remove from the heat and stir in the remaining ingredients. Pour into a 2-quart bowl or gelatin mold. Refrigerate and allow to set for at least 3 hours. When ready to serve, dip the mold in hot water, just covering the sides of the mold, for 10 seconds and invert quickly over a serving plate that is larger than the mold. Gently shake the mold to loosen it.

NOTE: This is a great addition to any buffet, and you can really have fun garnishing it with different fresh fruit each time you make it.

Summer Citrus Mold

6 to 8 servings

I'm convinced that a chilled gelatin go-along for a summer get-together is the perfect way to say, "It's summer and I'm loving it!"

1 package (4-serving size) lime-flavored gelatin
1 cup boiling water
½ cup half-and-half
½ teaspoon vanilla extract
½ cup sour cream
1 cup sliced strawberries
1 teaspoon lemon zest (see Note)

In a medium-sized bowl, dissolve the gelatin in the boiling water. Gradually stir in the half-and-half and vanilla. Add the sour cream and mix well. (The mixture will appear curdled.) Chill for 15 to 20 minutes, until slightly thickened. With an electric beater, beat until the mixture is smooth, then stir in the strawberries and lemon zest. Pour into a 9-inch pie plate and chill for 3 hours or until firm.

NOTE: What's lemon zest? Zest is the flavorful outside skin of citrus fruit. You can grate the citrus skin to get the zest, or it can be removed from the citrus with a gadget called a zester that's designed to remove the thin skin without going too deep and getting the bitter white skin.

Pot of Gold

12 to 14 servings

After a summer's rain we can often see a rainbow with lots of beautiful colors. Do they really end in a pot of gold? Make this rainbow go-along and maybe you'll find out. . . .

1 package (4-serving size) strawberry-flavored gelatin
1 package (4-serving size) orange-flavored gelatin
3 cups boiling water, divided
1 cup cold water
1 package (4-serving size) lemon-flavored gelatin
¼ cup sugar
½ cup orange juice
1 can (8 ounces) pineapple tidbits, drained
1 container (8 ounces) frozen whipped topping, thawed

Prepare the strawberry and orange gelatins separately by dissolving each in 1 cup boiling water; stir until completely dissolved. Add ½ cup cold water to each, then pour each into a separate 8-inch square pan. Chill for about 1½ hours or until firm, then cut into 1-inch cubes. Cover and set aside in the refrigerator. Dissolve the lemon gelatin and sugar in 1 cup of boiling water and stir in the orange juice; chill until slightly thickened (about 30 minutes). Stir in the pineapple tidbits and whipped topping; mix well. Fold in the gelatin cubes and pour into a 10-inch tube pan. Chill for 6 to 8 hours or until firm. When ready to serve, dip the tube pan three quarters of the way up the sides in hot water for 10 seconds and invert quickly over a serving plate that is larger than the pan. Gently shake to loosen from the pan. Cut into ½-inch slices.

   Mr. Food®'s "take-along" suggestion

Chicken Potato Salad

4 to 6 servings

Everybody loves chicken salad, and everybody loves potato salad. Here's an easy way to combine two favorites.

4 boneless, skinless chicken breast halves (1 to 1¼ pounds)
5 medium-sized red potatoes, cooked and cut into 1-inch cubes
3 tablespoons pickle relish
1 cup mayonnaise
3 tablespoons Worcestershire sauce
1 small red onion, chopped (about ½ cup)
¼ teaspoon salt
¼ teaspoon pepper

Fill a medium-sized saucepan halfway with water and bring to a boil; add the chicken breasts, reduce the heat to medium-low, and cook for 10 to 12 minutes or until no pink remains. Drain the water, pat the breasts dry with a paper towel, and allow to cool; cut the chicken into small chunks, place in a medium-sized bowl, and stir in the potatoes. In a small bowl, blend the remaining ingredients, then toss with the chicken and potatoes until evenly coated. Serve immediately or cover and chill until ready to use.

NOTE: It's easy to create a crunchy version of this salad—just add ½ cup drained sliced water chestnuts along with the chicken and potatoes and garnish it with 2 chopped scallions.

B.L.T. Salad

6 servings

B.L.T. Salad? Sound crazy? I thought so, too, but I tried making it anyway . . . and am I glad! Yup, it tastes just like a B.L.T. sandwich on toast. It's the answer for a quick, light lunch get-together.

1 medium-sized head of iceberg or romaine lettuce, shredded (about 8 cups)
2 large tomatoes, chopped (about 2 cups)
1 pound bacon, cooked until crisp, crumbled
2 cups seasoned croutons
¾ cup mayonnaise
¼ cup milk
1 teaspoon garlic powder
¼ teaspoon salt
¼ teaspoon pepper

Place the lettuce on the bottom of a large salad bowl. Layer over that the tomatoes, crumbled bacon, and croutons. In a blender on medium-high speed, blend the mayonnaise, milk, garlic powder, salt, and pepper. Just before serving, pour the dressing over the salad but don't toss it! (That'll ruin its super look.)

NOTE: Dig down to the bottom of the bowl when serving, so you'll be sure to have some of each layer in every portion.

Shrimp Scampi Salad

6 to 8 servings

Wouldn't it be nice to serve up a big platter of shrimp scampi to your crowd? Sure it would—but the price wouldn't be so nice. So I came up with this less-expensive salad that has a great "pricey" taste!

8 ounces uncooked pasta rings or small shells
¾ cup mayonnaise
1 tablespoon chopped fresh parsley
2½ teaspoons garlic powder
1 tablespoon lemon juice
1 teaspoon salt
½ teaspoon white pepper
1 package (10 ounces) frozen cooked shrimp,
thawed and drained

In a large pot of boiling salted water, cook the pasta according to the package directions; drain, rinse, drain again, and set aside. In a large bowl, combine the mayonnaise, parsley, garlic powder, lemon juice, salt, and pepper; blend until smooth. Add the pasta and shrimp to the mayonnaise mixture and toss to blend. Cover and refrigerate for at least 1 hour before serving.

NOTE: Don't forget to have a few varieties of crackers on hand.

Cheesy Hot Chicken Salad

9 to 12 servings

Is there a rule about all salads having to have lettuce or all salads having to be served cold? Nope! Here's the proof... and you can put away all those dressing bottles because you won't need them with this!

4 cans (5 ounces each) chunk-style chicken, drained and flaked
¾ cup chopped celery (2 to 3 stalks)
1 can (5 ounces) sliced water chestnuts, drained
1⅓ cups mayonnaise
2 tablespoons grated onion
2 tablespoons lemon juice
3 cups (12 ounces) grated Cheddar cheese, divided
1 cup crushed corn flakes

Preheat the oven to 350°F. In a medium-sized bowl, combine the chicken, celery, water chestnuts, mayonnaise, onion, lemon juice, and 2 cups of the cheese; mix well. Place the mixture in a 9" × 13" baking dish that has been coated with nonstick vegetable spray. Bake for 25 to 30 minutes or until hot. Sprinkle the remaining cheese evenly over the chicken and top with the crushed corn flakes. Bake for 3 to 5 more minutes or until the cheese melts.

NOTE: Serve with crusty bread for a warm salad lunch on a chilly day.

Taco Salad

12 servings

I first tried this at a potluck picnic. Boy, was it fun trying all the different salads! Everybody went crazy for this one, so why not make it for your next backyard picnic?

1 pound ground beef
1 package (1¼ ounces) dry taco seasoning mix
1 medium-sized head of iceberg lettuce, chopped (about 8 cups)
2 cups (8 ounces) shredded Cheddar cheese
1 can (16 ounces) kidney beans, rinsed and drained
2 large tomatoes, diced (about 2 cups)
2 cans (2.25 ounces each) sliced black olives, drained
1 bag (14½ ounces) ranch-flavored tortilla chips, crushed
1 bottle (16 ounces) sweet-and-spicy French salad dressing

In a medium-sized skillet, brown the ground beef with the taco seasoning mix, stirring to break up the meat; drain and cool. In an extra-large salad bowl, layer half of the lettuce, then half of the cheese, beans, ground beef, tomatoes, and olives. Repeat the layers once more, then top with the crushed tortilla chips. Before serving, add the dressing and toss well to coat.

NOTE: It's a complete meal in one bowl. Just bring out the paper plates, forks, and a jug of lemonade, and you're set!

Asian Baked Chicken Salad

6 to 8 servings

Are you ready for a change from traditional lunch salads? I bet this one'll be a welcome change.

2 tablespoons vegetable oil
6 boneless, skinless chicken breast halves (1½ to 1¾ pounds)
1½ cups chopped celery (3 to 4 stalks)
1 cup chopped pecans
½ teaspoon salt
½ teaspoon pepper
1½ cups mayonnaise
2 tablespoons lemon juice
1½ cups chow mein noodles (about 3 ounces)

Preheat the oven to 350°F. In a large skillet, heat the oil over medium heat and cook the chicken breasts for 10 to 12 minutes until lightly browned on both sides. Cut into 1-inch chunks and place in a large bowl. Add the remaining ingredients except the chow mein noodles; mix well. Pour into an 8-inch square baking dish. Sprinkle the chow mein noodles evenly over the top, cover with aluminum foil, and bake for 20 minutes. Uncover and bake for 15 minutes more, until the top is golden.

NOTE: Add a crisp garden salad and a loaf or two of crusty French bread . . . and you're set!

Tortellini Romaine Salad

5 to 6 servings

Mama mia! Are you used to being stuck in the kitchen when you have company? You won't be when you make this dish.

1 bag (16 ounces) frozen cheese tortellini
1 package (10 ounces) frozen green peas
½ of a medium-sized head of romaine lettuce,
cut into bite-sized pieces
1 jar (2 ounces) chopped pimientos (¼ cup), drained
½ teaspoon pepper
½ cup Caesar salad dressing

Cook the tortellini according to the package directions, stirring in the peas during the last 3 minutes of boiling. Drain, rinse under cold water, and drain well. Place the tortellini and peas in a large bowl and add the lettuce, pimiento, and pepper. Pour the dressing over the mixture and toss until evenly coated. Serve immediately.

NOTE: If you'd prefer a chilled salad, then cover and refrigerate the tortellini after cooking, and toss it with the remaining ingredients just before serving.

Reuben Salad

6 servings

One bowl, one quick toss, and you'll think you're in a New York deli. Pass the pickles, please!

4 cups shredded cabbage (½ of a small head)
¾ pound coarsely chopped cooked corned beef (2¼ cups)
1 cup (4 ounces) shredded Swiss cheese
1 bottle (8 ounces) Thousand Island dressing

In a large bowl, combine all of the ingredients except the dressing; cover and chill until ready to use. Toss with the dressing just before serving.

NOTE: You should be able to get a piece of whole corned beef from the supermarket deli department. And if you want to keep costs down, ask for the end pieces. They'll chop up just as well!

Column A Chicken Salad

6 to 8 servings

Most Chinese restaurants have menus set up so that you can choose from meals in different columns. There's usually one column that has all my favorite choices... and this Chinese-flavored salad sure is number one with me!

2 cups water
4 boneless, skinless chicken breast halves (about 1 pound)
4 cups shredded iceberg lettuce (½ of a small head)
4 cups shredded red cabbage (½ of a small head)
½ cup sliced scallions (about 3 scallions)
¼ pound snow peas, ends trimmed, halved
1 medium-sized red bell pepper, seeded and cut into julienne strips

Dressing
5 tablespoons vegetable oil
2 teaspoons sesame oil
¼ cup soy sauce
3 tablespoons cider vinegar
½ teaspoon garlic powder
¼ teaspoon black pepper

In a medium-sized saucepan, bring the water to a boil. Add the chicken and reduce the heat to medium. Cook for 15 to 20 minutes or until the chicken is cooked through. Remove the chicken from the water, pat dry with paper towels, and allow to cool. Slice the cooled chicken crosswise into ¼-inch strips and place in a large salad bowl. Toss in the lettuce, cabbage, scallions, snow peas, and red pepper. In a small bowl, whisk together the dressing ingredients until well mixed. Pour the dressing over the salad and toss immediately before serving.

Caribbean Stacked Salad

10 to 12 servings

Went shopping and forgot to get lettuce? Don't worry. You can still make this salad by layering other fresh veggies and topping them with a Caribbean dressing. Poof! Your salad worries are gone!

2 medium-sized zucchini, cut into 1-inch chunks
4 medium-sized yellow squash, cut into 1-inch chunks
2 medium-sized red bell peppers, cut into 1-inch chunks
8 ounces fresh green beans, trimmed and blanched
3 medium-sized sweet onions, cut into 1-inch chunks, divided
2 medium-sized cucumbers, cut into 1-inch chunks
3 to 4 medium-sized tomatoes, cut into 1-inch chunks
6 large radishes, thinly sliced

Dressing
1 pint (16 ounces) sour cream
¼ cup lemon juice
½ teaspoon salt
½ teaspoon white pepper

Place the zucchini chunks in a large glass bowl; layer with the yellow squash, red peppers, green beans, half of the onions, and the cucumbers. Top with the tomatoes. Place the sour cream, lemon juice, salt, pepper, and remaining onions in a food processor; process until liquefied. When ready to serve, pour half of the dressing over the top of the vegetables, reserving the other half to use as needed. Top the dressed salad with the sliced radishes or cover and chill until ready to serve. Then top with the dressing and radishes.

   Mr. Food®'s "take-along" suggestion

Roast Beef Sandwich Salad

8 to 10 servings

"Hmm... Should I serve a platter of sandwiches or maybe just a hearty salad?" Why not a salad that tastes like an overstuffed roast beef sandwich? They'll love it—and you!

Horseradish Dressing
1 cup mayonnaise
½ cup sour cream
3 tablespoons prepared horseradish, drained
½ teaspoon pepper
½ teaspoon salt
3 tablespoons olive oil

2 medium-sized heads of romaine lettuce,
torn into bite-sized pieces
1 pound thick-sliced roast beef, cut into ½-inch-wide strips
½ of a medium-sized red onion, sliced (about ½ cup)
2 medium-sized tomatoes, chopped
2 cups seasoned croutons

In a medium-sized bowl, combine the dressing ingredients; mix well and set aside. Place the remaining ingredients, except the croutons, in a large bowl; toss to mix. Pour the dressing over the salad and toss to coat well. Stir in the croutons and serve.

"Pumped Up" Potato Salad

8 to 10 servings

This is a really neat way to "pump up" your salad. I wonder why we didn't think of it before now!

6 large white potatoes
2 cans (6 ounces each) tuna in water, drained and flaked
1 cup chopped celery (2 stalks)
½ cup chopped red bell pepper
⅓ cup chopped scallions (1 to 2 scallions)
2 cups mayonnaise
1 tablespoon white vinegar
1 teaspoon dried dill
½ teaspoon salt
½ teaspoon white pepper

Place the potatoes in a large pot and add just enough water to completely cover them. Bring to a boil and cook for 35 to 40 minutes or until the potatoes are fork-tender; drain and cool. Peel the potatoes and cut into 1-inch chunks; place the chunks in a large bowl and add the remaining ingredients. Mix until the potatoes are completely coated. Cover and chill for at least 2 hours before serving.

NOTE: If you want, you can even cook the potatoes a day before making the salad—this will cut down on the time needed to chill the salad before serving.

Shrimp Cocktail Salad

8 to 10 servings

Entertaining on the patio, by the pool, or in the backyard? I've got just the side salad for you—or is it a main course? Hmm...

1 medium-sized head of iceburg lettuce, thinly sliced
(about 8 cups)
2 cans (4.25 ounces each) shrimp, drained
¾ cup cocktail sauce

In a large bowl, combine the lettuce, shrimp, and cocktail sauce. Toss until the lettuce and shrimp are evenly coated. Serve immediately or cover and chill until ready to use.

NOTE: Serve each portion on a plate or in a stemmed glass, maybe with a lemon wedge.

Crowd-Sized
Sandwiches and Breads

A sandwich can be the main attraction of a party! How about serving a giant one at your next backyard get-together? Serve an Explosive Deli Torpedo (page 194) or Antipasto Gondola Sandwiches (page 196). And if a few extra guests show up, so what?! Just cut these jumbo sandwiches a little smaller. Nobody will know but you.

Buffalo wings are so "in" now—everybody loves 'em! You've got to try Buffalo Chicken Salad Sandwich (page 193). You won't believe how it captures the taste of the real thing.

This started out as a sandwich chapter only, but since we need bread to make sandwiches, I figured I'd add some breads here, too. And these breads are super! Piñata Bread (page 198) is studded with smoked meats and veggies, and State Fair Herb Bread (page 199) is a real prize winner.

There are lots more . . . and these sandwiches and breads go a long way, so when you invite the group over or when the gang just stops by, how 'bout breaking bread with them? They'll surely feel like family.

CROWD-SIZED SANDWICHES AND BREADS

Mr. Food®'s "take-along" suggestion

Baked Reuben

12 servings

You remember that favorite deli of yours that served Reubens piled high with corned beef and sauerkraut and smothered in cheese? Wouldn't it be nice to serve those at your next casual get-together? They're easy! (And don't forget the pickles!)

1 loaf (12 ounces) French bread, unsliced
1 bottle (8 ounces) Russian or Thousand Island dressing (1 cup)
12 ounces sliced corned beef
1 can (14.4 ounces) sauerkraut, well drained
1 package (6 ounces) sliced Swiss cheese

Preheat the oven to 400°F. Cut the bread in half lengthwise (horizontally) and slightly hollow out each half by removing the soft center ½ inch deep on each side. Fill each hollowed-out half with ¼ cup of the dressing. Place half of the corned beef on each half of the loaf and spoon another ¼ cup of the dressing over the corned beef. Top each half evenly with the sauerkraut, followed by half of the cheese. Wrap each half loosely in aluminum foil and bake for 20 minutes, until the cheese melts. Cut each half into 6 pieces.

NOTE: You can use rye bread instead of French bread if you'd rather, but it tends to be a bit harder to cut and eat.

Portobello Mushroom "Steak-out"

10 to 12 servings

*Portobello mushrooms seem to be popping up a lot on our produce depart-
ment shelves. Have you tried them yet? Come on! Made this way they taste
like grilled steak sandwiches!*

6 tablespoons (¾ stick) butter
2 to 3 medium-sized onions, chopped (about 2 cups)
8 ounces Portobello mushrooms, stems on, cut into
⅛-inch-thick slices (4 to 5 medium-sized mushrooms)
¼ cup bottled steak sauce
1 loaf (8 to 10 ounces) French bread, cut in half lengthwise
1 package (6 ounces) sliced provolone cheese

Preheat the broiler. In a large skillet, over medium-high heat, melt
the butter and sauté the onions for 6 to 8 minutes, until softened.
Add the mushrooms, reduce the heat to medium, and continue cooking for 3 to 5 more minutes, turning often. Pour the steak sauce over
the onions and mushrooms and stir. Divide the mixture evenly over
the French bread halves and top with the cheese slices. Broil for 5
to 8 minutes or until the cheese melts and the top is golden. Use a
serrated knife to cut diagonally into serving-sized pieces.

Jumbo Italian Meat Loaf Sandwich

6 servings

Have you ever tried to bite into a meatball sandwich and had the meatballs roll out and splatter all over you? I think I've found the solution!

1¼ pounds ground beef
½ cup Italian-style bread crumbs
2 eggs
2 tablespoons grated Parmesan cheese
1 teaspoon salt
¼ teaspoon pepper
1⅓ cups spaghetti sauce, divided
1 loaf (1 pound) Italian bread, unsliced
2 tablespoons olive oil
½ teaspoon garlic powder
½ cup (2 ounces) shredded mozzarella cheese

Preheat the oven to 350°F. In a large bowl, combine the ground beef, bread crumbs, eggs, Parmesan cheese, salt, and pepper; mix well. Place the mixture on a large rimmed cookie sheet that has been coated with nonstick vegetable spray and form into a loaf the size of the bread. Bake for 30 minutes, then remove the meat loaf from the oven and spread ⅓ cup of the spaghetti sauce over the top. Bake for 20 to 25 more minutes or until cooked through. Meanwhile, slice about ¾ inch off the top of the bread. Hollow out the loaf, leaving ½ inch of bread around the edges of the crust. Brush with the olive oil and sprinkle with the garlic powder. Place on another rimmed cookie sheet and bake for 10 minutes. When the meat loaf is done, place it inside the bread shell; pour the remaining sauce on top and sprinkle with the mozzarella cheese. Bake for 7 to 8 minutes or until the cheese is melted and the sauce is hot. Replace the top of the bread and cut into slices.

NOTE: Serve with additional warm spaghetti sauce, if you'd like.

Buffalo Chicken Salad Sandwich

6 to 8 servings

I used to serve the guys batches of chicken wings when they came over to watch ball games. They were so messy that I had to find a way to keep that great Buffalo taste, but without all the bones and napkins.

8 boneless, skinless chicken breast halves (about 2 pounds)
½ cup chopped celery (1 stalk)
½ cup blue cheese salad dressing
2 teaspoons hot pepper sauce
½ teaspoon paprika
1 loaf (12 to 16 ounces) French bread

Preheat the oven to 350°F. Place the chicken in a 9" × 13" glass baking dish. Cover with aluminum foil and bake for 20 to 30 minutes or until the chicken is cooked through and the juices run clear. Let cool, then coarsely chop. Place in a large bowl and add the celery, dressing, hot pepper sauce, and paprika; mix well. Slice the French bread in half lengthwise and hollow out the bottom half, leaving ½ inch of bread around the edges of the crust. Fill with the chicken salad and cover with the top half of the loaf. Slice into serving-sized portions and serve.

NOTE: For an authentic Buffalo taste, chop the celery a bit on the chunky side.

 Mr. Food®'s "take-along" suggestion

Explosive Deli Torpedo

6 to 8 servings

I use this as my secret weapon for drop-in company. It's my approach to world peace 'cause it makes everybody happy!

1 loaf (12 to 16 ounces) French bread
2 tablespoons olive oil
½ teaspoon garlic powder
8 ounces thinly sliced deli-style ham
8 ounces thinly sliced turkey breast
1 large tomato, thinly sliced
4 ounces thinly sliced Genoa or hard salami
4 ounces sliced mozzarella cheese

Preheat the oven to 350°F. Slice the bread lengthwise in half. Brush both cut sides with the olive oil and sprinkle evenly with the garlic powder. Layer the ham, turkey, tomato, salami, and cheese across each cut side. Cover with the other half of the bread and wrap tightly with aluminum foil. Bake for 20 to 25 minutes or until hot. Slice into serving-sized portions and serve.

NOTE: I suggest cutting this with a serrated knife—it'll hold together better.

Layered Sandwiches

12 to 14 servings

No more hearing, "I want this!" "No, I want that!" Serve everybody a slice of this combo sandwich, and they'll have a chance to sample everything!

1 loaf (1 pound) bakery white bread, unsliced
1 can (6 ounces) tuna fish, drained
½ cup mayonnaise, divided
½ teaspoon dried dill
4 ounces (½ of an 8-ounce package) cream cheese
¼ cup chopped green olives with pimientos
4 hard-boiled eggs, chopped
3 tablespoons drained sliced black olives (about
½ of a 2.25-ounce can)
¼ teaspoon salt
⅛ teaspoon pepper

Turn the bread on its side lengthwise. Slice a ¾-inch slice from the bottom. Slice off 2 more slices of the same size so that the bread is in 4 equal long pieces; set aside. In a small bowl, combine the tuna, ¼ cup mayonnaise, and dill. In another small bowl, combine the cream cheese and green olives. In a third small bowl, mix together the eggs, the remaining mayonnaise, olives, salt, and pepper. Spread each of the fillings evenly on a separate layer of the bread, then stack the layers on top of one another. Cover the layers with the top of the loaf. Slice the loaf as you would a loaf of bread, each slice about ¾ inch thick, and serve.

NOTE: With a bag of chips and an assortment of pickles, you've got a super luncheon buffet!

Antipasto Gondola Sandwiches

6 to 8 servings

A gondola is an Italian boat similar to a canoe—and that's what this finished sandwich looks like, with its hollowed-out Italian bread brimming with the makings of an Italian antipasto.

1 loaf (1 pound) Italian bread, unsliced
2 cups shredded iceberg lettuce
4 ounces thinly sliced Genoa salami
1 large tomato, thinly sliced
1 package (6 ounces) sliced provolone cheese
¾ cup roasted peppers, drained and patted dry
1 can (2.25 ounces) sliced black olives, drained (½ cup)
6 pepperoncini, tops removed, sliced in half and seeded
¼ cup thinly sliced red onion
¼ teaspoon dried oregano
2 tablespoons Italian dressing

Slice the bread in half lengthwise. Carefully hollow out the bottom half of the loaf. Place the lettuce in the hollow and then layer the salami, tomato, cheese, roasted peppers, olives, pepperoncini, and onion. Sprinkle with the oregano. Just before serving, pour on the Italian dressing. Cover with the other half of the loaf and slice into serving-sized portions.

NOTE: This should hold together while cutting if you use a serrated knife.

Seafood Roll-ups

14 tortilla rolls

Roll 'em up and dish 'em out... What an easy way to entertain!

2 pounds imitation crabmeat, finely chopped (about 4 cups)
1 package (1 ounce) ranch salad dressing mix
2 scallions, chopped (about ¼ cup)
1 can (2.25 ounces) sliced black olives, drained (½ cup)
1 cup mayonnaise
Fourteen 7-inch soft flour tortillas
1 large tomato, chopped (about 2 cups)
¼ of a head of iceberg lettuce, shredded

In a large bowl, combine the imitation crabmeat, salad dressing mix, scallions, olives, and mayonnaise; mix well. Place ⅓ cup of the mixture in the center of each tortilla. Top with 1 tablespoon of the chopped tomato. Sprinkle the lettuce evenly over the tomato on the tortillas. Roll up the tortillas and serve.

Piñata Bread

6 to 8 servings

Take out the party hats and noisemakers 'cause slice after slice of this hearty bread yells, "Let's party!"

1 loaf (1 pound) frozen white bread dough, thawed
¼ cup diced cooked ham
1 tablespoon diced red onion
2 tablespoons diced red bell pepper
2 tablespoons diced green bell pepper
1 tablespoon diced jalapeño pepper (1 whole pepper, seeded)
½ teaspoon Italian seasoning
1 tablespoon dry taco seasoning mix
¼ cup shredded Monterey Jack cheese

On a lightly floured board, roll out the thawed bread dough to 8" × 11". Layer the dough with the remaining ingredients. Roll up the dough, jelly-roll fashion, tucking in the ends as you roll, and place seam side down in a 9-inch loaf pan that has been coated with nonstick vegetable spray. Cover with a damp cloth and allow to rise for 1 hour. Heat the oven to 375°F. and bake for 30 minutes or until golden brown. Cool before slicing.

NOTE: This is great rewarmed—just put it into a 200°F. oven for 15 to 20 minutes and WOW!

State Fair Herb Bread

6 to 8 servings

A blue ribbon winner at the fair and a gold medal winner on your buffet table!

1 large package (17.3 ounces) refrigerated buttermilk biscuits
(8 biscuits), cut into sixths
1 small package (10.8 ounces) refrigerated buttermilk biscuits
(5 biscuits), cut into sixths
2 teaspoons dried parsley flakes
1 teaspoon dried basil
½ teaspoon garlic powder
½ teaspoon salt
¼ teaspoon pepper
1 tablespoon butter, melted

continued

Preheat the oven to 350°F. Place the cut-up biscuits in a large bowl and top with the remaining ingredients except the butter. Toss until the biscuits are evenly coated. Add the melted butter and toss again. Place in a 9-inch loaf pan that has been coated with nonstick vegetable spray and bake for 40 to 45 minutes or until golden brown. Let cool for 10 minutes and invert the loaf pan over a serving plate.

NOTE: Serve with room-temperature creamy butter.

Peanut Butter and Jam Bread

12 slices

Yes, the title says it . . . peanut butter and jam are baked right into this bread. So all you have to do is cut and enjoy!

2 cups all-purpose flour
½ cup sugar
1 tablespoon baking powder
1 teaspoon salt
¾ cup peanut butter
1 egg, slightly beaten
1 cup milk
½ cup strawberry or grape jam or preserves

Preheat the oven to 350°F. In a large bowl, combine the flour, sugar, baking powder, and salt. Cut the peanut butter in with an electric mixer until well combined. Add the egg and milk; stir until well blended. Spread half the batter into a 9-inch loaf pan that has been coated with nonstick vegetable spray and top with the jam. Cover the jam with the remaining batter and bake for 55 to 60 minutes or until a wooden toothpick inserted in the center comes out clean. Invert onto a wire rack and let cool before slicing.

NOTE: This is a great snack that the kids'll love, and why not try spreading each slice with a tablespoon or two of marshmallow creme!

Everyday Fruit Loaf

8 to 10 servings

At holiday time we feel like we have to have fruitcake—and we always have leftovers. Well, this fruit loaf is different . . . watch how fast it disappears!

1 cup raisins
1 cup dried apricots, quartered
2 teaspoons baking soda
1½ cups sugar
¼ teaspoon ground cinnamon
½ cup (1 stick) butter
1 cup boiling water
2 eggs, slightly beaten
2½ cups all-purpose flour

Preheat the oven to 350°F. In a large bowl, combine the raisins, apricots, baking soda, sugar, cinnamon, and butter. Add the boiling water; mix well. Let cool, then add the eggs and flour. Mix by hand until moistened; the batter will be lumpy. Pour into a loaf pan that has been coated with nonstick vegetable spray and bake for 75 to 85 minutes or until a wooden toothpick inserted in the center comes out clean.

NOTE: The finished loaf should be very moist.

 Mr. Food®'s "take-along" suggestion

Kid Stuff

This chapter is for our toughest food critics—our kids. Kids sure do let us know exactly how they feel when it comes to food, don't they (especially if they're picky eaters)?

And of course kids like to have fun. Mealtime can be fun, too! I've put together a bunch of easy recipes that are not only fun to eat, like Spaghetti Sundaes (page 206) and Farmers' Chicken Fingers (page 209), they're fun to make, too, like Mice Creams (page 214) and Baseball Mitts (page 216). Yes, I'm talking about letting your kids help in the kitchen. What better time for them to learn than when they're young and full of enthusiasm? Sure, they're going to make a mess, but that's how they learn. They can even make some Play Clay (page 219) to play with when they finish preparing their food. Of course, young children should never be allowed in the kitchen unsupervised. They need you there to teach them the proper ways to handle food and utensils. (I bet *you* learn a thing or two, too!)

So, let the kids enjoy cooking with you and **Mr. Food**®. And if you're good, maybe they'll share their Itsy Bitsy Pizza Bagels (page 210) with you!

KID STUFF

Mr. Food®'s "take-along" suggestion

Cooking with Kids

What kid doesn't like to help Mom or Dad, big brother or sister in the kitchen? Sure, not only do they like to eat their creations, they love to help make them, too. But before getting started, please review these simple rules with your little ones to ensure big smiles and, yup, of course lots of **"OOH IT'S SO GOOD!!™"**

- Always have adult supervision when using knives, appliances, and the stove top and oven.
- Wash hands before starting.
- Read the ingredients list and help check that everything is available.
- Have Mom or Dad preheat the oven, if needed.
- Be a good helper by working alongside Mom or Dad, and help measure, mix, and prepare foods according to the recipes.
- Show Mom and Dad how creative you are by making special recipes like Mice Creams (page 214) and Baseball Mitts (page 216).
- Make sure Mom or Dad uses pot holders when putting pans in and taking pans out of the oven. Never do this by yourself.
- Clean up the counters and dirty dishes.
- Always wrap and store foods properly with adult supervision.

Spaghetti Sundaes

8 servings

Tell the kids that they're having sundaes for dinner and watch their faces. Oh, yes—they're spaghetti sundaes. And don't forget the "cherry" on top of each one . . . you know, I mean meatballs!

1 pound uncooked spaghetti
1 jar (16 ounces) spaghetti sauce

Meatballs
¾ pound ground beef
⅓ cup Italian-style bread crumbs
1 egg
½ teaspoon salt
¼ teaspoon pepper

Preheat the oven to 350°F. In a large pot of boiling water, cook the spaghetti according to the package directions; drain, rinse, and drain again. In a medium-sized saucepan, heat the spaghetti sauce over low heat until heated through. Meanwhile, in a large bowl, combine the meatball ingredients; mix well. Form into 8 meatballs and bake on a large rimmed cookie sheet that has been coated with nonstick vegetable spray for 20 to 25 minutes. Toss the spaghetti in the sauce until evenly coated and place in sundae glasses. Top each with a meatball and serve.

NOTE: How 'bout putting out a bowl of grated Parmesan cheese for them to sprinkle on top of their sundaes? It'll make it kind of like a sundae bar.

Crispy Honey Chicken

3 to 4 servings

This has two things that kids love—a crispy crunch and a touch of sweetness. That sure makes it fun, too!

2 cups cornflake crumbs
1 cup honey
1 chicken (2½ to 3 pounds), cut into 8 pieces

Preheat the oven to 350°F. Place the cornflake crumbs in a shallow bowl; set aside. Place the honey in another shallow bowl and dip the chicken into the honey until well coated. Dip the chicken into the cornflake crumbs, completely coating the chicken. Place in a 9" × 13" glass baking dish that has been coated with nonstick vegetable spray and bake for 50 to 55 minutes or until golden brown and cooked through.

Fun on a Bun

6 to 8 servings

The name says it all—there's a barrel of fun in every bite.

1½ pounds ground beef
2¼ cups spaghetti sauce
2 teaspoons light brown sugar
1 cup crushed tortilla chips
6 to 8 hamburger buns

In a large skillet, brown the ground beef over medium-high heat for about 8 minutes, stirring occasionally; drain any excess liquid. Stir in the remaining ingredients except the buns. Reduce the heat to low and simmer for 8 to 10 minutes, until heated through. Serve on the hamburger buns.

NOTE: What a great last-minute throw-together when you've got a hungry gang on your hands!

Farmers' Chicken Fingers

4 to 5 servings

These really aren't the fingers of a chicken—they're just long strips of chicken. The only fingers here are the tiny ones that grab them off the plate and gobble them up!

4 boneless, skinless chicken breast halves (1 pound)
1 bag (6 ounces) potato chips, crushed
½ cup ranch salad dressing

Preheat the oven to 400°F. Slice the chicken lengthwise into ½-inch strips. Place the crushed potato chips in a shallow bowl; set aside. Place the salad dressing in a shallow bowl and dip the chicken into the dressing, shaking off any excess. Dip the chicken into the crushed potato chips, completely coating the chicken. Place on a cookie sheet that has been coated with nonstick vegetable spray and bake for 15 to 20 minutes or until the chicken is cooked through.

NOTE: My grandchildren like dipping these in ketchup. I like sweet-and-sour and barbecue sauce for mine.

Itsy Bitsy Pizza Bagels

20 mini-pizzas

Your kids will be in their glory when you tell them they're going to make their own individual pizzas. Ask them which is more fun—making them or eating them!

1 bag (9 ounces) frozen miniature bagels, thawed
½ cup pizza or spaghetti sauce
1 cup (4 ounces) shredded mozzarella cheese
20 slices pepperoni (1 ounce) or 1 jar (2.5 ounces) mushroom stems and pieces, drained

Preheat the oven to 350°F. Split the bagels in half and spread 1 teaspoon sauce on each half. Then sprinkle each half with 1 heaping teaspoon mozzarella cheese and 1 slice of pepperoni or mushroom and place on a foil-lined cookie sheet. Bake for 10 to 12 minutes or until the cheese is melted.

NOTE: Before baking these, you can wrap them well and freeze for later use. When you want to bake them, just take them right from the freezer and lay them on a foil-lined cookie sheet. Pop them in a 350°F. oven for 12 to 15 minutes and they'll be ready!

Chefs-in-Training Cake

2 dozen squares

This simple cake is perfect for young chefs-in-training. With a little supervision, your miniature cooks can be kitchen heroes, too!

1 can (20 ounces) crushed pineapple, drained, with juice reserved
1 can (20 to 21 ounces) cherry pie filling
1 box (18.25 ounces) white cake mix
1 cup flaked coconut
1 cup (2 sticks) butter, melted
1 cup chopped walnuts

Preheat the oven to 350°F. Spread the pineapple and pineapple juice on the bottom of a 9" × 13" baking dish. Place the pie filling over the pineapple, then spread the *dry* cake mix on top. Sprinkle with coconut and drizzle with the melted butter. Top with the chopped walnuts. Bake for 1 hour or until the sides are bubbling and the top is browned.

NOTE: Let the cake cool for about an hour before cutting. This is super for a slumber party! Just serve with scoops of ice cream on the side.

  Mr. Food®'s "take-along" suggestion

Dreamsicles

6 servings

These treats will make the gang feel really special. After all, everybody thinks it takes a lot of work to make homemade ice cream on a stick. (If they only knew how easy these are ... Shh!)

3 cups orange juice
1 can (5 ounces) evaporated milk
½ cup sugar
1 tablespoon vanilla extract
5 drops red food color (optional)

Blend all of the ingredients in a blender or in a large bowl with an electric mixer until the sugar has completely dissolved. Pour into popsicle molds and freeze until solid.

NOTE: Don't lose your cool if you don't have popsicle molds: it's the stick part that the kids love, anyway. You can use just about any freezer-safe container to make homemade frozen treats. Try using small plastic cups and non-toxic wooden craft sticks—or even plastic spoons—for your handles. The cups are perfect for catching drips or for "keeping the rest for later" when their sweet tooth is larger than their appetite.

Waffle S'mores

6 to 8 servings

No, these aren't really for breakfast, but your kids will wish they were! They're great for a special treat when you've got a bunch of kids visiting.

1 package (8 ounces) frozen waffles (8 waffles)
1 cup semisweet chocolate chips
16 large marshmallows

Preheat the oven to 350°F. Place 4 waffles on an ungreased cookie sheet. Sprinkle ¼ cup of the chocolate chips, then 4 marshmallows on each waffle. Top each with another waffle. Bake for 12 to 14 minutes or until the chocolate chips and the marshmallows are melted and the waffles are crisp. Cut each in half and serve immediately.

NOTE: You could turn this into a fun party activity—with adult supervision, of course.

Mice Creams

6 servings

When you get done, I bet these look like expensive store-bought desserts. They're not—and the best part is that the kids can all help with the decorating (after they wash their hands, of course).

1 pint vanilla ice cream
1 package (4 ounces) single-serve graham cracker crusts
(6 tart shells)

Ears
12 chocolate fudge mint cookies or chocolate wafers

Tails
Six 3-inch strands of black shoestring licorice

Eyes and Noses
18 brown chocolate-coated candies

Whiskers
2 teaspoons chocolate sprinkles

Put 1 scoop of vanilla ice cream into each tart shell. Tuck two cookie "ears" and a "tail" into the ice cream. Press the "eyes," "noses," and "whiskers" in place. Cover loosely with plastic wrap and freeze until ready to serve.

NOTE: Don't limit your kids' creativity. Have lots of fun toppings to help them create their own treats.

Baseball Mitts

6 servings

Want a home run treat for the little leaguers and their families? Serve these after the game to make any team feel like a winner.

1 package (4 serving-size) any flavor instant pudding
and pie filling
2 cups milk
1 package (4 ounces) single-serve graham cracker crusts
(6 tart shells)

Balls
1½ cups frozen whipped topping, thawed

Fingers
12 Vienna Finger sandwich cookies

Stitching on Balls
1 tube (.68 ounce) red decorating gel

Prepare the pudding with the 2 cups milk as directed on the package. Spoon into the tart shells. Spoon the whipped topping over the pudding and edge of crust to cover, smoothing the surface and mounding it to resemble a baseball. Break each sandwich cookie in half crosswise. Tuck 3 broken halves into the pudding in each shell, slightly overlapping them around the upper edge of the shells, to resemble the fingers of a baseball mitt. Put another half cookie slightly to the left of the other "fingers," making "thumbs." Draw two half circles and stitching on the "balls" with the gel.

NOTE: Store in the refrigerator, loosely covered with plastic wrap.

Surprise Sundae Cups

1 dozen cups

Here's a great new twist on an old favorite. They're like ice cream cupcakes with a surprise center. Boy, will the kids love these!

1 quart chocolate or vanilla ice cream
12 miniature milk chocolate peanut butter cup candies
¼ cup semisweet chocolate chips, melted
¼ cup chopped walnuts

Line a 12-cup muffin tin with paper liners; place ⅓ cup ice cream in each cup. Press a candy into the center of each cup of ice cream, so that the candy is completely covered with ice cream. In a small saucepan, melt the chocolate chips over very low heat, stirring just until melted. Remove the saucepan from the heat immediately. Drizzle about 1 teaspoon of the melted chips, then 1 teaspoon of the chopped walnuts over each ice cream cup. Cover the muffin tin and place it in the freezer for at least 3 to 4 hours.

NOTE: If you let the kids eat these with plastic spoons, they'll feel like they've got walk-away ice cream surprises!

Play Clay

17½ ounces

This is one recipe that is made to be played with, NOT TO BE EATEN! It's ideal for a rainy day indoor activity.

1 cup all-purpose flour
½ cup salt
2 tablespoons cream of tartar
1 cup water
2 teaspoons any color food color

In a medium-sized saucepan, combine all of the ingredients. Stir and cook over medium heat for 2 to 3 minutes. Remove from the heat and let cool. Remove from the pan, scraping down the sides of the pan, and knead until the color is evenly distributed. It can be used immediately.

NOTE: To keep this soft, store it in a resealable plastic bag when the kids finish playing with it. To firm it up after making jewelry or simple artwork, you can bake the finished pieces in a 350°F. oven for 10 minutes or until firm to the touch.

   Mr. Food®'s "take-along" suggestion

Ice Breakers

If you do what I used to do and serve soda or beer to someone who stops by, why not decide to add a little personality and sparkle to your beverages? Whether you serve drinks with or without alcohol, there are so many great choices!

My Bloody Mary (page 225) recipe is perfect for brunch, and so are Secret Mimosas (page 226). So many of us enjoy them when we go out for brunch. They're so simple, why shouldn't we make them at home? (You'll wonder why you didn't try making them before now!)

And if you want to share the tastes of the Caribbean, try cool, refreshing Nonalcoholic Frozen Piña Coladas (page 230). Or maybe take your guests south of the border with Nonalcoholic Strawberry Margaritas (page 229).

And let's not forget thick and frosty milk shakes! They're an all-American tradition, and once you try my Memory Lane Milk Shake (page 234) and Brown Cow Milk Shake (page 235) recipes, your gang will insist that you make them a regular tradition at *your* house—starting immediately!

Serving the right drinks will help your party or get-together be a smooth success. That's right—you're going to be a kitchen hero again!

ICE BREAKERS

Mr. Food®'s "take-along" suggestion

Beverage Tips

I've got a super selection of drinks in this chapter—something for everybody. But before you decide which specialty drinks to make for your next party, check out these general tips. They should help with your planning, which should make your party go a lot smoother.

1. The first decision you need to make is how extensive you want your beverage selection to be, and whether or not you want to serve alcoholic drinks and both cold and hot beverages.

2. As far as how much to buy, my rule of thumb is this: For each hour of the get-together, plan on having about 1 to 1½ drinks per person. So for a 4-hour party, you would plan on 5 to 6 drinks per person—no, all of those drinks shouldn't contain alcohol. You know your guests best, so plan the amount of drinks accordingly.

3. Always make sure to have some alcohol-free choices and diet drinks on hand for those who prefer them. Sparkling waters and flavored seltzers are really popular now. And having a punch like Graduation Punch (page 228) is an easy, festive way to make sure that there's an alcohol-free option.

4. You might choose to serve only wine and beer, which certainly simplifies things by limiting choices (and it makes shopping a lot easier). Just be sure to have red and white wine, maybe even a blush type for a broader selection, as well as regular, light, and nonalcoholic beer.

5. For a full bar at a party, you should have these liquors on hand: vodka, gin, whiskey, rum, scotch, and bourbon. If you'd like a bigger selection, you could add tequila and even cordials

or after-dinner drinks like coffee-, nut-, and mint-flavored liqueurs. But remember, the more choices there are, the bigger the variety of mixers you'll need. What do I mean by "mixers"? Tonic water, club soda, water, and also regular and diet types of cola, lemon-lime, and ginger ale sodas. And don't forget a selection of fruit juices including orange, tomato, cranberry, and grapefruit as well as lemons, limes, oranges, and everybody's favorite, maraschino cherries, for garnishing.

6. Don't forget the ice! Plan on having 1 pound of ice for every guest. That's for adding to drinks; you'll need additional ice for keeping beer, wine, and sodas cool in an ice chest, if that's how you'll be storing those. You can save money by planning ahead and making the ice yourself. Just make batches of ice cubes and pop them out of the trays into plastic storage bags that you keep in your (or a friend's) freezer. When you're entertaining outdoors in the summertime, remember that ice melts quickly, so plan on extra for those occasions.

7. If you really want to get fancy, before you freeze your ice cubes, cut small pieces of lemon or lime and place them in the water in the ice cube trays. It looks super and will flavor the drinks as the cubes melt.

8. You can make ice cubes from fruit juices, too, and use them in your favorite drinks. That way, when the ice melts, it won't water down the drinks while it keeps them nice and cold.

9. I sure do like my beverages frosty cold, so remember to add ice just before serving and, if possible, have all of the drink ingredients chilled, too!

10. For bigger bashes, why not make ice molds to dress up your punch bowl? They sure are easy to make. Just fill a 10-inch Bundt pan or gelatin mold with water or juice (or a combination) and add some slices of citrus fruit. (You can even add

sliced fresh strawberries.) Freeze the mold till it's solid. Then simply unmold it and gently place it in the punch bowl just minutes before your guests arrive. It looks great. (Oh, yes, when you put the punch in the bowl, remember to leave plenty of extra room for the ice mold!)

11. If you serve alcohol, please be a responsible host. Don't let anyone overdo it, and certainly don't let your guests drink and drive. Stop serving alcohol toward the last part of your get-together. That's a good time to change to coffee and other nonalcoholic beverages. When your guests arrive you can ask them to assign one designated driver per vehicle. I've also heard of hosts collecting guests' car keys when they arrive and giving them back at the end of a party only if they're sure their guests can drive themselves home safely. The next day you sure want to hear lots of raves about your party—you know, like **"OOH IT'S SO GOOD!!™"**

Bloody Mary

6 servings

If you want to add a bit of spice to your brunch, this drink should liven things up. It's the perfect eye-opener for the sleepy brunch gang.

1 can (46 ounces) tomato juice
3 tablespoons lime juice
1 tablespoon Worcestershire sauce
1½ teaspoons prepared white horseradish, drained
1 teaspoon hot pepper sauce
¾ teaspoon salt
½ teaspoon pepper
¾ cup vodka (optional)
6 celery stalks, trimmed and cleaned
Ice cubes

In a large covered jar or pitcher, combine all of the ingredients except the celery and ice. Shake or mix well, until evenly blended. Place the celery stalks and some ice cubes in tall glasses. Pour the Bloody Mary mixture over the ice and serve.

NOTE: This can be easily doubled or tripled and served in a punch bowl for larger morning gatherings.

 Mr. Food®'s "take-along" suggestion

Secret Mimosas

8 to 10 servings

If you want to serve something really classy that doesn't take much work, here you go! But since it's so easy, let's keep the recipe a secret. After all, our guests don't have to know we didn't fuss for them!

2 quarts orange juice, chilled
1 bottle (750 ml) champagne or sparkling wine, chilled
1 orange, thinly sliced

In a large pitcher, combine the orange juice and champagne. Immediately pour into champagne or wine glasses. Garnish with the orange slices.

NOTE: For a nonalcoholic version of this brunch favorite, mix the orange juice with sparkling apple juice instead of champagne.

Whiskey Sour Punch

6 servings

Whenever I think of whiskey sours, I think of the glamorous stars of the '30s and '40s. Drinking this won't turn you into a movie star, but it deserves its own awards!

1 large can (12 ounces) frozen lemonade concentrate
4 cups cold water
1¼ cups whiskey
6 maraschino cherries

In a blender, combine half of each of the ingredients except the cherries, and blend on high speed until thoroughly mixed. Pour into a punch bowl over ice and repeat with the remaining frozen lemonade, water, and whiskey. Add the cherries and serve.

NOTE: Because of the whiskey, this drink is for adults only. If you want to make a nonalcoholic icy lemonade punch, simply replace the whiskey with water.

Graduation Punch

15 to 20 servings

The first time I made this was for a friend's graduation party. It's nonalcoholic and packed full of refreshing fruit juice. You'll certainly receive high honors for serving it!

1 large can (12 ounces) frozen fruit punch drink
concentrate, thawed
1 small can (6 ounces) frozen orange juice
concentrate, thawed
1 small can (6 ounces) frozen lemonade
concentrate, thawed
2 liters ginger ale
1 quart orange sherbet

In a large punch bowl, combine the fruit punch, orange juice, and lemonade concentrates. Stir until well mixed. Add the ginger ale and orange sherbet and refrigerate until ready to serve.

NOTE: For a really festive look, slice up a few oranges, lemons, and/or limes to float on top of the punch.

Nonalcoholic Strawberry Margaritas

5 to 6 servings

Serve these in sugar-rimmed glasses. How do you do that? Turn your tall drinking glasses upside down in ¼ inch of water, then dip the rims in granulated sugar. Pop them securely in the freezer for 1 to 2 hours. Fill them up and let the party begin!

> 1 large can (12 ounces) frozen limeade concentrate
> 1½ cups cold water
> ⅓ cup sugar
> 1 package (16 ounces) frozen whole strawberries
> 1 to 2 cups ice cubes (depending on your desired
> drink consistency)

Combine all of the ingredients in a large blender. Blend until well mixed and thick. Pour ¾ cup of the margarita mixture into each of 5 to 6 tall glasses and serve immediately.

NOTE: If you'd like, add ¼ to ⅓ cup of tequila to the blender for the tropical alcohol version. (Rum is okay, too.)

Nonalcoholic Frozen Piña Coladas

5 to 6 servings

You want tropical? I'll give you tropical! You do have to supply your own palm trees and ocean breezes, but the rest is in your glass!

2¼ cups pineapple juice
½ cup flaked coconut
3 cups vanilla ice cream
Maraschino cherries (optional)

Combine all of the ingredients except the cherries in a large blender. Blend until thick and well mixed. Serve immediately in stemmed glasses garnished with maraschino cherries, if desired.

NOTE: If you want it frostier, add 1 cup of ice cubes (8 to 10 ice cubes) before blending. And if you dare to add rum, add ⅓ cup light or dark rum to the rest of the ingredients in the blender and give it a whirl.

St. Patrick's Day Cocktails

4 to 6 servings

It used to be that I made this drink only in honor of St. Patrick's Day. But my friends insisted they didn't want to wait another whole year for it, so I gave in, and now they can enjoy it any time of the year!

1 can (14 ounces) sweetened condensed milk
1½ cups heavy cream
4½ teaspoons chocolate-flavored syrup
¾ cup Irish or other whiskey

Combine all of the ingredients in a blender and blend on medium speed until thoroughly mixed. Cover and refrigerate until ready to serve, then mix again and serve over ice in cordial glasses or juice-sized glasses.

NOTE: This drink can be made ahead of time and stored, covered, in the refrigerator for up to 2 weeks. For a thick, rich Irish milk shake, add a scoop or two of vanilla ice cream and blend until smooth.

   Mr. Food®'s "take-along" suggestion

Frozen Lemonade Cooler

6 to 8 servings

This is a great new frozen way to serve a lemonade-like drink. It'll take you back to those lazy hot summer days of yesteryear...

2 cups lemon sherbet
1 small can (6 ounces) frozen lemonade concentrate
3 cups water
1 teaspoon lemon zest (see page 171)

Combine all of the ingredients in a blender and blend on high speed for 20 to 30 seconds or until smooth and creamy. Serve immediately.

Hot Mulled Fruit Cider

12 to 16 servings

Wow! This is the perfect drink for those cold winter nights in front of the fireplace with friends and family. Hopefully, it'll keep them warm and cozy all the way home, too!

1 large can (12 ounces) frozen apple juice concentrate, thawed
1 large can (12 ounces) frozen cranberry juice concentrate, thawed
1 small can (6 ounces) frozen lemonade concentrate, thawed
10 cups water
½ cup light or dark rum
5 cinnamon sticks
7 whole cloves
1 teaspoon ground nutmeg

Place the frozen apple juice, cranberry juice, and lemonade concentrates in a large saucepan. Add the water and mix thoroughly. Add the remaining ingredients and simmer over medium-low heat for 15 to 20 minutes.

NOTE: Serve in heat-resistant cups or mugs garnished with extra cinnamon sticks. And of course you can leave out the rum if you'd prefer a nonalcoholic version.

Memory Lane Milk Shake

5 servings

Boy, oh boy, will this milk shake remind you of bobby socks and saddle shoes! You'll think you've gone back in time to a '50s soda fountain!

2½ cups vanilla ice cream
2 cups frozen strawberries (about ⅔ of a 16-ounce package)
1¼ cups milk
½ cup sugar
5 whole fresh strawberries, cleaned

Combine all of the ingredients except the fresh strawberries in a blender. Blend on high speed until smooth. Pour into tall glasses and top each with a fresh strawberry.

NOTE: These are so thick that you'll need to serve them with straws *and* spoons!

Brown Cow Milk Shake

5 to 6 servings

Smooth, creamy, and delicious, this is a shake that's perfect teamed with a cheeseburger and a big plate of fries. For your next Friday night get-together, introduce your friends to your brown cows.

3 cups chocolate ice cream
1½ cups milk
½ cup chocolate-flavored syrup

Combine all of the ingredients in a blender and blend for 1 to 1½ minutes or until the mixture is smooth and thick.

NOTE: If you prefer a thinner shake, use an additional ½ cup milk.

Bananas 'n' Cream Daiquiri

4 to 5 servings

There's no question—you'd better plan on making a double batch 'cause they'll be lining up for seconds!

1 small can (6 ounces) frozen lemonade concentrate,
slightly thawed
3 large ripe bananas
1½ cups water
2 cups ice cubes
1 cup frozen whipped topping, thawed
½ cup light rum (optional)

Place all of the ingredients in a blender and blend until thick and well mixed. Turn off the blender and scrape down the sides; continue blending if necessary.

NOTE: If you like your blender drinks really thick, plan ahead: Cut the bananas into 1-inch pieces and freeze them in a resealable plastic storage bag. Use them while still frozen.

Yogurt Smoothie

6 servings

This drink has it all—it looks super, the taste is even better, and it's nutritious. The best part is that it's so yummy, no one would ever guess how healthy it is!

2 cans (8 ounces each) pineapple chunks,
with ½ cup juice reserved
1 can (16 ounces) pears, with ½ cup juice reserved
1 cup frozen strawberries
3 tablespoons sugar
1 cup plain yogurt
1 cup ice cubes

Combine all of the ingredients except the ice in a blender; blend until smooth. Blend in the ice cubes until smooth, and serve.

NOTE: The great thing about this drink is that you can use whatever fruit you happen to have in the house—canned, frozen, or fresh. It all works!

Sweet Good-byes

Oh, boy! It's time to plan dessert! And, let me tell you, there's so much here, you won't know what to make first!

Peanut Butter Cup Cake with Peanut Butter Drizzle (page 250) is a winner every time, and so are Drop-in Ice Cream Sandwiches (page 268). Do you need something big for a big group of people? Bring out the Texas Sheet Cake (page 246). And for a really fun treat, what about Chocolate Almond Frozen Bananas (page 261) and Cherry Cola Parfaits (page 269)? Or how about Cinnamon Breakfast Ring (page 253)? It's so much fun to pull the pieces off the ring when you want just a nibble. . . . Mmm!

Now don't get nervous! All of these taste super, and they're super easy to make, too. From Stacked Black Forest Cake (page 241) to light and fancy Almond Crunch Custard (page 248), one of them is the perfect topper for your special event.

Good luck. . . . Oh, I don't mean that you need luck to *make* these. You'll need luck trying to *choose* just one or two to share!

SWEET GOOD-BYES

Mr. Food®'s "take-along" suggestion

Mr. Food®'s "take-along" suggestion

Stacked Black Forest Cake

6 to 8 servings

As they bite through layer after layer, your friends will applaud this new version of a dessert classic. Yup, this cake will stack up against any other dessert.

One 1-pound chocolate pound cake
1 container (8 ounces) frozen whipped topping, thawed
1 package (8 ounces) cream cheese, softened
¼ cup confectioners' sugar
1 can (20 to 21 ounces) cherry pie filling

Slice the pound cake lengthwise into thirds. In a medium-sized bowl, combine the whipped topping, cream cheese, and confectioners' sugar; beat with an electric mixer until smooth. Place the bottom layer of cake on a serving platter and spread with one third of the topping mixture. Spread one third of the pie filling over the topping mixture and place the middle layer of cake over it. Repeat the layers, ending with pie filling on top. Cover and chill for 1 hour or until ready to serve.

NOTE: For the neatest slices, cut this with a serrated knife.

Ultimate Chocolate Chunks

3 to 4 dozen cookies

Serving fresh-from-the-oven chocolate chip cookies is an open invitation that company truly welcomes!

2 cups all-purpose flour
1 teaspoon baking soda
½ teaspoon salt
½ cup (1 stick) butter, softened
½ cup vegetable shortening
½ cup granulated sugar
¾ cup firmly packed brown sugar
1 teaspoon vanilla extract
1 egg
1 package (12 ounces) semisweet chocolate chunks (2 cups)
½ cup chopped nuts (optional)

Preheat the oven to 375°F. In a medium-sized bowl, combine the flour, baking soda, and salt; set aside. In a large bowl, combine the butter, shortening, sugars, and vanilla; beat until creamy. Beat in the egg, then gradually add the flour mixture, mixing well. Stir in the chocolate chunks and nuts with a wooden spoon; mix well. Drop by rounded teaspoonfuls 2 inches apart onto ungreased cookie sheets. Bake for 8 to 10 minutes. Cool on cookie sheets for 2 minutes, then remove cookies to a wire rack to cool completely.

All-in-One Carrot Cake

2 dozen squares

I was in a restaurant recently where I saw a mom who was desperate to get her son to eat some carrot sticks. I have a feeling he would have eaten his carrots this way. Do you think I could make it work with broccoli?

2 cups granulated sugar
1½ cups vegetable oil
4 eggs
2 teaspoons baking soda
2 cups all-purpose flour
2 teaspoons ground cinnamon
1 teaspoon salt
1 cup flaked coconut
3 cups grated carrots (about 1 pound carrots)
1 cup chopped walnuts

continued

 Mr. Food®'s "take-along" suggestion

Preheat the oven to 350°F. In a large bowl, combine all of the ingredients and blend with an electric mixer until a smooth, thick batter forms. Pour the batter evenly into a 9" × 13" baking dish that has been coated with nonstick baking spray. Bake for 40 to 45 minutes or until a wooden toothpick inserted in the center comes out clean and the top and sides are golden brown. Let cool completely, frost with cream cheese frosting (see below), and cut into squares.

Cream Cheese Frosting

1 package (8 ounces) cream cheese
1 cup (2 sticks) butter, softened
1 teaspoon vanilla extract
1 box (16 ounces) confectioners' sugar

In a large bowl, with an electric mixer, mix the cream cheese and butter. Add the vanilla and mix well. Gradually add the confectioners' sugar, continuing to mix until well combined. Use this to top a cooled All-in-One Carrot Cake or other cakes. If making the frosting in advance, cover and keep chilled. Let the frosting sit out at room temperature for 30 minutes before using.

Caramel Frozen Squares

10 to 12 servings

Ice cream desserts are perfect for company because they can be in the freezer, ready when we need them. So, be ready to wow the neighbors with this treat the next time they stop by.

1½ cups firmly packed light brown sugar
½ cup evaporated milk
7 tablespoons butter, melted, divided
½ teaspoon vanilla extract
1 package (17 ounces) pecan shortbread cookies
½ gallon vanilla ice cream, softened

In a small saucepan, combine the brown sugar and evaporated milk over medium-low heat and bring to a boil. Reduce the heat to low and simmer the sauce for 2 to 3 minutes, stirring constantly until the sugar is totally dissolved. Remove from the heat and stir in 1 tablespoon of butter and the vanilla; set aside to cool. In a food processor, process the cookies to the consistency of medium-coarse crumbs. Set aside 1½ cups of the crumbs. In a medium-sized bowl, combine the remaining crumbs with the remaining melted butter. Press the crumb mixture into the bottom of a 9" × 13" baking dish that has been lightly coated with nonstick baking spray. Pour three quarters of the sauce over the crumb crust. Carefully cover with the ice cream. Evenly drizzle the remaining caramel sauce over the ice cream. Top with the reserved 1½ cups of cookie crumbs. Cover and freeze for at least 3 hours or until firm. Let soften for 5 to 10 minutes. Cut into squares and serve.

Texas Sheet Cake

28 to 32 servings

I've heard that everything in Texas is big. Maybe that's the reason for this recipe's name—it's big for serving a crowd and it's got big taste for loads more "OOH IT'S SO GOOD!!™" pardner."

Cake
2 sticks (1 cup) butter
1 cup water
¼ cup cocoa powder
2 cups all-purpose flour
2 cups granulated sugar
2 eggs
½ cup sour cream
1 teaspoon baking soda
½ teaspoon salt

Frosting
¼ cup (½ stick) margarine
3 tablespoons milk
2 tablespoons cocoa powder
1 box (16 ounces) confectioners' sugar
½ teaspoon vanilla extract

In a small saucepan over low heat, combine the butter, water, and ¼ cup cocoa powder. Remove from the heat and pour into a large

 Mr. Food®'s "take-along" suggestion

heat-resistant bowl. Allow to cool, then add the remaining cake in-gredients and beat together until mixed. Pour into a 10"×15" rimmed cookie sheet and bake for 25 minutes, until a knife inserted in the center comes out clean; set aside to cool. Meanwhile, make the frosting by melting the margarine, milk, and 2 tablespoons cocoa powder in a small saucepan over low heat. Remove from the heat and stir in the confectioners' sugar and vanilla. Mix well. When it's cool, ice the cake, using a spatula.

NOTE: Do you want to fancy this up a bit? Sprinkle the frosting with crushed chocolate sandwich cookies, broken-up pieces of your favorite chocolate candy bar, or Texas-sized whole shelled walnuts!

Almond Crunch Custard

6 to 8 servings

Wait—does this recipe belong with dessert or pasta? The only way to know for sure is to taste it. Okay, I'll give you a hint... You'll love it at the end of a meal.

½ cup uncooked orzo or Rosamarina pasta
2 eggs
1 cup milk
½ cup firmly packed light brown sugar, divided
¼ cup granulated sugar
¼ cup all-purpose flour
¼ cup (½ stick) plus 1 tablespoon butter, softened, divided
1½ teaspoons vanilla extract
½ cup slivered almonds

Preheat the oven to 350°F. Cook the orzo according to the package directions; drain and set aside. In a blender, combine the eggs, milk, ¼ cup of the light brown sugar, the granulated sugar, flour, ¼ cup of the butter, and the vanilla; blend on medium speed for 1 to 2 minutes. Place the mixture in a large bowl, then fold in the cooked orzo. Pour into a 9-inch deep-dish metal pie plate that has been coated with nonstick baking spray and bake for 35 to 40 minutes or until set. Meanwhile, in a small bowl, combine the remaining ¼ cup light brown sugar and 1 tablespoon butter, and the slivered almonds. Sprinkle over the custard and broil for 2 to 3 minutes, until bubbly and golden brown. Let cool before serving, or cover and chill until ready to use.

Corner Store Orange Favorite

10 to 12 servings

Remember the ice cream novelties we used to get at the corner store? Well, this creamy orange treat reminds me of my favorite snack from those days.

2 packages (4 servings each) orange-flavored gelatin
3 cups boiling water
1 quart orange sherbet
1 cup (½ pint) heavy cream

Place the gelatin in a large bowl and add the boiling water; stir until the gelatin is dissolved. Add the sherbet and stir until it melts into the gelatin mixture; set aside. In a medium-sized bowl, whip the heavy cream with an electric beater for 7 to 10 minutes, until light and fluffy. Fold the whipped cream into the sherbet mixture and pour into a 10-inch Bundt pan. Refrigerate overnight to set. When ready to serve, remove from the pan: Dip the pan in a warm water bath for a few minutes—but be careful not to get any water in the pan. Invert onto a plate, remove pan, and cut into slices.

Peanut Butter Cup Cake

10 to 12 servings

It's happening again . . . it is! It started with combining chocolate and peanut butter in candy. It followed in cookies, then in ice cream—where there were big chunks or gobs of both chocolate and peanut butter. Now it's time for these two popular flavors to meet again in a moist cake.

1 box (18.25 ounces) devil's food cake mix
1 package (4-serving size) instant chocolate pudding and pie filling
1 cup (½ pint) sour cream
1 cup vegetable oil
4 eggs
½ cup water
30 miniature milk chocolate peanut butter cup candies, crushed

Preheat the oven to 350°F. In a large bowl, with an electric beater, combine all the ingredients except the crushed candies; mix well. Stir in the crushed candies and mix well. Pour into a well-greased 10-inch Bundt pan and bake for 60 to 65 minutes or until a wooden toothpick inserted in the center comes out clean. Cool the cake slightly, about 15 minutes. Remove the cake from the pan and continue to cool thoroughly on a wire cooling rack.

Peanut Butter Drizzle

Enough for 1 Bundt cake or a 2-layer cake

½ package (5 ounces) peanut butter chips
6 large marshmallows
⅓ cup evaporated milk (½ of a 5-ounce can)

In a medium-sized saucepan, combine all of the ingredients over low heat and stir until the sauce is melted and smooth. Immediately drizzle over Peanut Butter Cup Cake or your favorite chocolate or vanilla cake.

Ugly Cake

10 to 12 servings

When I first turned this cake out of the pan, I didn't think I was going to like it—it didn't look very good. Well, I went for it—and the taste was incredible! So I gave it a whole new look by topping it with dollops of whipped topping and some gummy worms. Now it tastes great and looks great (and the kids just love it)!

1 can (21 ounces) blueberry pie filling
1 package (18.25 ounces) yellow cake mix
2 eggs
2 tablespoons vegetable oil
1 teaspoon vanilla extract
½ cup chopped walnuts
1 cup frozen whipped topping, thawed
Gummy worms, for garnishing

Preheat the oven to 350°F. In a blender, purée the blueberry pie filling until smooth. In a large bowl, combine the pie filling, cake mix, eggs, oil, and vanilla; beat with an electric mixer for about 2 minutes on medium speed. Stir in the walnuts and pour into a 10-inch Bundt pan that has been coated with nonstick baking spray. Bake for 50 to 55 minutes, until a wooden toothpick inserted in the center comes out clean. Cool slightly, then remove from the pan and continue cooling on a wire cooling rack. Before serving, top with dollops of whipped topping and decorate with gummy worms.

NOTE: I usually use walnuts here, but shelled pecans and pistachios give it a different delicious taste!

Cinnamon Breakfast Ring

6 to 8 servings

I know this says it makes 6 to 8 servings, but the first time I made this I almost ate the whole cake by myself... well, I didn't, and I don't recommend trying that. Instead, find some very good friends to share it with, because it's special enough for the best people in your life.

1 large package (17.3 ounces) refrigerated buttermilk biscuits
(8 biscuits)
1 small package (10.8 ounces) refrigerated buttermilk biscuits
(5 biscuits)
1 tablespoon butter, melted
½ cup granulated sugar
2 teaspoons ground cinnamon
½ cup raisins
½ cup chopped walnuts
½ cup confectioners' sugar
4 teaspoons milk

Preheat the oven to 350°F. Separate the large can of biscuit dough into 8 biscuits and the small can into 5 biscuits. Cut each biscuit into 6 pieces and place the pieces in a large bowl. Pour the melted butter over the biscuit pieces. In a small bowl, combine the granulated sugar, cinnamon, raisins, and nuts. Sprinkle the sugar mixture over the biscuit pieces and toss until evenly coated. Place the dough into a 10-inch Bundt pan that has been coated with nonstick baking spray. Bake for 30 to 35 minutes or until the center is firm.

continued

Let cool for 10 to 15 minutes, then invert the Bundt pan over a plate to release the cinnamon ring. In a small bowl, combine the confectioners' sugar and milk to make a glaze; drizzle over the ring and serve immediately.

NOTE: The best way to eat this is to pull it apart. Not only is it tasty, but it's fun to eat!

Neighborhood
Blueberry Coffee Cake

15 servings

On my recent book tour, a viewer brought me a recipe that she said was the hit of her neighborhood. When I got home I just had to try it. Know what? Now it's the hit of my neighborhood, too!

1 cup (2 sticks) butter
1½ cups sugar
3 eggs
3 cups all-purpose flour
2 teaspoons baking powder
1 teaspoon vanilla extract
1 can (21 ounces) blueberry pie filling

Topping
¼ cup all-purpose flour
¼ cup sugar
2 teaspoons butter
1 teaspoon ground cinnamon

Preheat the oven to 350°F. In a large bowl, cream the 1 cup butter and 1½ cups sugar. Add the eggs 1 at a time. Add the 3 cups flour, the baking powder, and vanilla; mix well. Spread half of the batter into a 9" × 13" metal baking pan that has been coated with non-stick baking spray. Using a wet knife, spread the pie filling evenly

 Mr. Food®'s "take-along" suggestion

over the batter and cover it evenly with the remaining batter. In a small bowl, mix together all of the topping ingredients with a fork until crumbly. Sprinkle over the batter and bake for 55 to 60 minutes or until a wooden toothpick inserted in the center comes out clean. Cool in the pan on a wire cooling rack. Cut and serve.

NOTE: If you use a glass baking dish, it will cook a little faster, so adjust your cooking time.

Cranberry Swirl Cake

10 to 12 servings

Lots of people only think of cranberries at Thanksgiving time. Not me! I like to enjoy their tangy taste all year long—and here's another great way to do that!

½ cup (1 stick) butter, softened
1¼ cups granulated sugar
2 eggs
2 cups all-purpose flour
1 teaspoon baking powder
1 teaspoon baking soda
½ teaspoon salt
1 cup (½ pint) sour cream
1½ teaspoons almond extract
½ cup chopped walnuts
1 can (8 ounces) whole-berry cranberry sauce, divided
1 tablespoon confectioners' sugar

Preheat the oven to 350°F. In a large bowl, cream the butter and granulated sugar together with an electric mixer. Add the eggs and beat until smooth. In a medium-sized bowl, combine the flour, baking powder, baking soda, and salt. Add to the creamed mixture and mix well. Add the sour cream, almond extract, and walnuts. Pour half of the batter into a 10-inch Bundt pan that has been coated with nonstick baking spray. Swirl in half of the can of cranberry sauce and cover with the remaining batter (see Note). Swirl the remaining cranberry sauce on top. Bake for 45 to 50 minutes or until a wooden toothpick inserted in the center comes out clean. Let cool for 20 minutes, then turn out onto a serving plate. When completely cool, sprinkle with confectioners' sugar.

NOTE: To swirl the cranberry sauce, drop out half of the sauce by tablespoonfuls onto the batter and swirl it through the batter with a butter knife.

Coffee Can Cake

12 to 16 slices

This is what I call a real "coffee" cake. It sure will perk up lots of interest at your party.

1 cup water
2 tablespoons instant coffee granules
½ cup raisins
1 teaspoon baking soda
1¼ cups sugar
¼ cup (½ stick) butter
½ teaspoon vanilla extract
1 egg
⅛ teaspoon ground cinnamon
2 cups all-purpose flour
¼ cup chopped walnuts

Preheat the oven to 350°F. In a small saucepan, combine the water, coffee, raisins, and baking soda. Bring to a boil and cook for 2 minutes, stirring constantly. Remove from the heat and allow to cool. In a medium-sized bowl, cream the sugar and butter. Add the vanilla, egg, and cinnamon. Alternately stir in the flour and the cooled raisin mixture, mixing well. Fold in the nuts, then divide the batter evenly between 2 coffee cans that have been coated with non-stick baking spray. Place both cans on a baking sheet and bake for 50 to 55 minutes or until a wooden toothpick inserted in the center comes out clean. Let cool for 15 minutes. Remove from the cans by opening the bottoms with a can opener and pushing the cakes out the tops of the cans, then slice.

NOTE: Since this recipe makes 2 cakes, why not freeze 1 right in the can with the plastic coffee can lid on top? Then you're ready for the coffee klatch.

Chocolate Almond Frozen Bananas

6 to 8 servings

A big favorite of yesterday was frozen bananas. They were sold at the ballpark, on the boardwalk, and even at the corner store. Now see how easy it is to make them right in your own kitchen!

6 to 8 bamboo skewers

3 to 4 large, ripe (but firm) bananas
1 package (12 ounces) semisweet chocolate chips
¼ cup vegetable shortening
1 teaspoon almond extract
¾ cup chopped almonds

Line a rimmed cookie sheet with waxed paper. Cut the bananas in half crosswise and place a skewer lengthwise through the center (beginning at the cut side) of each half. When all of the banana halves are skewered, place on the cookie sheet and freeze for 3 to 4 hours, or overnight. After the bananas have frozen, place the chocolate chips and shortening in a medium-sized glass bowl. Microwave on high for 1 to 2 minutes, just until the chips are melted. Remove from the microwave and mix until smooth. Add the almond extract and almonds; mix well. Over the bowl of chocolate, hold each banana by the stick and spoon the chocolate mixture over the banana, evenly coating it. Work fast because the chocolate hardens quickly. Allow the excess to drip off. Lay the coated bananas on the waxed paper and freeze for 45 minutes to 1 hour. Store in resealable plastic storage bags.

continued

NOTE: If you'd prefer to melt the chocolate on the stove top, just place the chocolate and shortening in a medium-sized saucepan and melt over low heat, stirring frequently. Do not allow the mixture to burn. If wrapped tightly, these bananas can last for up to 2 months in the freezer.

Anytime Cookie Balls

6 dozen cookie balls

Do you need a dessert that can go to school, to work, and even be ready to go when you get unexpected company? These will do all that! They're ready for anytime, anywhere (and they travel so well, too)!

1 cup (2 sticks) butter
2 cups all-purpose flour
¼ cup granulated sugar
1 cup shelled walnuts
1 cup flaked coconut
1 cup semisweet chocolate chips
½ teaspoon almond extract
¼ cup confectioners' sugar

Preheat the oven to 375°F. In a food processor, combine all of the ingredients except the confectioners' sugar. Pulse the mixture on and off until well blended. Form the mixture into bite-sized balls and place on an ungreased cookie sheet. Bake for 10 to 12 minutes, then allow to cool. Sprinkle with confectioners' sugar.

NOTE: These store well in an airtight container for up to 2 weeks, as long as you wait till they're completely cooled before storing.

    Mr. Food®'s "take-along" suggestion

Family-Sized Sundae

12 to 15 servings

It's great to have this on hand in the freezer when unexpected company drops by. Boy, will they be surprised!

½ gallon vanilla ice cream, divided
3 cups banana slices (3 medium-sized bananas), divided
1 jar (12 ounces) hot fudge sauce, warmed to
pourable consistency, divided
1 container (12 ounces) frozen whipped topping,
thawed and divided
½ cup chopped walnuts, divided
⅔ cup maraschino cherries (about 24 cherries), divided

Scoop half of the ice cream into balls and place in the bottom of a large bowl or trifle dish. Layer with 1½ cups banana slices, then spoon ½ cup of the hot fudge sauce over the bananas. Spread half of the whipped topping over that. Sprinkle ¼ cup walnuts and ⅓ cup cherries on top. Repeat the layers, then cover and freeze for at least 6 hours before serving. Remove from the freezer 10 to 15 minutes before serving.

Raspberry Banana Bonanza

6 servings

Options, options, options! Yup, that's what cooking is all about, and this recipe gives us a bonanza of choices. You can have it as a light, creamy mousse, or a frozen fruit cream—without changing the ingredients!

1 package (12 ounces) frozen raspberries
1 banana, peeled, cut into chunks, and frozen
3 cups frozen whipped topping, thawed
1 tablespoon rum (optional)
2 tablespoons sugar

Place the raspberries and the banana in a food processor with a cutting blade attachment. Process until the raspberries and banana are finely chopped. Add the remaining ingredients and process until smooth. Serve immediately as a light raspberry mousse. If you'd rather have a refreshing frozen fruit cream, place this in a plastic bowl, cover, and freeze until ready to serve. Soften slightly before serving, if desired.

NOTE: To freeze the banana, simply peel and cut it into 2-inch chunks. Place the chunks in a resealable plastic bag and place in the freezer for 1 to 2 hours.

Chocolate Sin

10 to 12 servings

We're always told not to sin, but I think we can make an exception with this treat.

One 1-pound chocolate pound cake, cut crosswise
into ¼-inch slices, divided
2 packages (4-serving size) instant chocolate pudding
and pie filling
3 cups milk
1 container (12 ounces) frozen whipped topping,
thawed and divided
1 cup chopped walnuts, divided
1¼ cups coarsely chopped chocolate sandwich cookies, divided

Layer half of the pound cake slices in a 9" × 13" glass baking dish. In a large bowl, combine the chocolate pudding mix and milk and blend with a wire whisk until thickened. Fold in half of the whipped topping. Place half of the mixture over the pound cake slices and sprinkle with ½ cup nuts and ½ cup cookie crumbs. Repeat the layers, then top with the remaining whipped topping and the remaining ¼ cup cookie crumbs. Cover and chill for 2 hours before serving.

NOTE: Since you're already sinning, you might want to stir a splash or two of your favorite chocolate-, coffee-, or fruit-flavored liqueur into the whipped topping when mixing it with the pudding.

   Mr. Food®'s "take-along" suggestion

Pineapple Right-Side-Up Cake

12 pieces

Pineapple Upside-Down Cake is really well known. No fair! Now it's time to get it right... right side up, I mean!

1 package (8 ounces) cream cheese, softened
¼ cup (½ stick) butter, softened
1¼ cups sugar
2 eggs
¼ cup milk
1 teaspoon vanilla extract
1¾ cups all-purpose flour
1 teaspoon baking powder
½ teaspoon baking soda
¼ teaspoon salt
1 jar (12 ounces) pineapple preserves
1 jar (10 ounces) maraschino cherries, drained and chopped

Preheat the oven to 350°F. In a large bowl, blend the cream cheese, butter, and sugar together with an electric mixer on high speed. Reduce the speed to low and add the eggs, milk, and vanilla; blend until smooth. Mix in the flour, baking powder, baking soda, and salt. Do not overmix. Pour half of the batter into a 9" × 13" baking dish that has been coated with nonstick baking spray. Spread the preserves evenly over the batter. Pour the remaining batter over the preserves. Sprinkle the chopped cherries evenly over the top and bake for 40 minutes or until a wooden toothpick inserted in the center comes out clean. Remove from the oven and let cool for 1 hour before cutting.

Drop-in Ice Cream Sandwiches

12 servings

Okay, so you won't hear the ice cream bell, but you will hear lots of "ooh"s and "ahh"s when you take this jumbo ice cream sandwich out of the freezer. It looks like it would be tricky to make, but it really takes just minutes!

1 package (16 ounces) chocolate sandwich cookies,
crushed (about 3 cups) (see Note)
⅓ cup butter, melted
½ gallon vanilla ice cream, slightly softened

Place the crushed cookies in a medium-sized bowl. Add the melted butter; mix well. Press half of the cookie mixture firmly into a 9" × 13" foil-lined baking pan. Spread the softened ice cream over the cookie mixture, then gently press the remaining cookie mixture over the ice cream. Cover and freeze for at least 6 hours. Cut into 12 sandwich squares.

NOTE: You can crush the sandwich cookies in a food processor or by placing them in a resealable plastic bag and rolling a rolling pin over them.

Cherry Cola Parfaits

6 to 8 servings

It used to be that you couldn't go into a diner without having a cherry cola. Here's how to get that same old-time taste and feel in a gelatin dessert.

2 packages (4 servings each) cherry-flavored gelatin
1⅔ cups boiling water
2 cups carbonated cola
1 cup chopped walnuts
1 cup chopped maraschino cherries
⅓ cup frozen whipped topping, thawed
3 plastic drinking straws, each cut in half

Place the gelatin in a large bowl and add the boiling water; stir until the gelatin is dissolved. Stir in the cola. Chill for about 45 minutes, then stir in the chopped walnuts and cherries. Divide the gelatin evenly into 6 to 8 dessert glasses (1 cup per glass) and chill for 2 to 3 hours or overnight. When ready to serve, top each with a dollop of whipped topping. Serve with the straws (just for fun).

NOTE: This is the perfect ending for a kids' meal of Fun on a Bun (page 208) and Smashed Potatoes (page 139).

Ice Cream Cone Cupcakes

24 cupcakes

One wants ice cream, one wants cake. Can't decide? Make these unique cupcakes in ice cream cones—and don't worry! They won't melt!

1 package (18.25 ounces) any flavor cake mix
24 flat-bottomed ice cream cones
½ cup candied sprinkles, divided
1 can (16 ounces) any flavor frosting

Preheat the oven to 350°F. Prepare the cake mix according to the package directions. Place the ice cream cones in cupcake tins and spoon 1 tablespoon of cake batter into each cone. Add 1 teaspoon of sprinkles over the batter, then cover with another tablespoon of batter. Bake for 25 to 30 minutes or until a wooden toothpick inserted in the center comes out clean. When cooled, spread with frosting.

NOTE: Instead of sprinkles, use ½ cup of crushed chocolate sandwich cookies, semisweet chocolate chips, or even hot fudge!

Triple Chocolate Cream Pie

10 to 12 servings

Chocolate in the crust, chocolate in the filling, and chocolate on top! Watch out, chocolate lovers, this could be addicting. You'd better serve it with a pitcher of ice cold milk.

1 package (12 ounces) semisweet chocolate chips
1 container (12 ounces) frozen whipped topping, thawed
⅓ cup milk
One 9-inch chocolate graham cracker pie crust
3 chocolate sandwich cookies, finely crushed (see Note)

In a medium-sized saucepan, melt the chocolate chips over medium heat, stirring constantly. Remove from the heat and let cool for 10 minutes. Place the whipped topping in a large bowl and, with an electric mixer, beat the melted chocolate into the topping, a little bit at a time, until completely blended. Add the milk and continue to beat until thoroughly mixed. Spoon into the crust and sprinkle the crushed cookie crumbs over the top. Refrigerate for 2 to 3 hours, until set.

NOTE: You can crush the sandwich cookies in a food processor or by placing them in a resealable plastic bag and rolling a rolling pin over them.

Frozen "Watermelon"

10 to 12 servings

It's not what you think—it's a frozen ice cream mold that looks like a watermelon when it's sliced . . . with chocolate chip "seeds" and everything! Tell your gang that it's okay to eat the seeds and even the rind of this watermelon!

> 3 pints vanilla ice cream, slightly softened
> ½ cup miniature semisweet chocolate chips
> 3 pints raspberry sherbet
> 14 drops green food color
> 2 cups frozen whipped topping, thawed

Line an 8-cup mold or mixing bowl completely with aluminum foil. Quickly spread the vanilla ice cream on the bottom and sides of the bowl, until it's about 1 inch thick. (It's okay that it slides down the sides a bit.) Immediately place back in the freezer for about 1 hour.

After the vanilla ice cream has become somewhat hard, but not frozen solid, rework it and spread it all the way up the sides to the top edges of the bowl; then replace it in the freezer for about 1 hour or until firm. Then, in a medium-sized bowl, add the chocolate chips to the raspberry sherbet and blend until evenly mixed. Place the raspberry mixture over the vanilla ice cream. Cover with plastic wrap and freeze overnight or until completely hard. When ready to serve, mix the green food color with the whipped topping until evenly blended. Take the mold out of the freezer and invert it over a platter larger than the mold. Remove the mold and peel back the foil. Spread the whipped topping evenly over the top of the ice cream and serve immediately or freeze until ready to serve. Cut into slices, just like watermelon.

Rich Snacking Fudge

64 pieces

If you're like me, you've got a weakness for snack food like potato chips and pretzels. And when they're added to creamy rich fudge, they taste like expensive chocolate-dipped pretzels and chips like the ones we see in fancy candy stores.

1 package (12 ounces) semisweet chocolate chips
1 can (14 ounces) sweetened condensed milk
1 teaspoon vanilla extract
2 cups coarsely crumbled potato chips *or*
1 cup coarsely crumbled pretzels

In a medium-sized saucepan, melt the chocolate chips over medium-low heat, stirring constantly. Be careful not to burn. When the chocolate is melted, reduce the heat to low and add the sweetened condensed milk and vanilla; stir until well blended. Remove from the heat and immediately add the crumbled potato chips or pretzels. Stir gently to blend and pour into an 8-inch square baking dish that has been coated with nonstick baking spray. Cover and cool in the refrigerator until set.

NOTE: I cut these into 1-inch squares because they're so rich and satisfying.

   Mr. Food®'s "take-along" suggestion

Index

Mr. Food®

Can Help You Be A Kitchen Hero!

Let **Mr. Food**® make your life easier with

Quick, No-Fuss Recipes and Helpful Kitchen Tips for

Family Dinners   Soups and Salads   Pot Luck Dishes
Barbecues   Special Brunches   Unbelievable Desserts

...and that's just the beginning!

Complete your **Mr. Food**® cookbook library *today.*

It's so simple to share in all the

"OOH IT'S SO GOOD!!™"